Vítor Pochmann

Diet Algorithms

Vítor Pochmann

Diet Algorithms

A mathematical view of the food problem

ScienciaScripts

Imprint
Any brand names and product names mentioned in this book are subject to trademark, brand or patent protection and are trademarks or registered trademarks of their respective holders. The use of brand names, product names, common names, trade names, product descriptions etc. even without a particular marking in this work is in no way to be construed to mean that such names may be regarded as unrestricted in respect of trademark and brand protection legislation and could thus be used by anyone.

Cover image: www.ingimage.com

This book is a translation from the original published under ISBN 978-620-6-75807-5.

Publisher:
Sciencia Scripts
is a trademark of
Dodo Books Indian Ocean Ltd. and OmniScriptum S.R.L publishing group

120 High Road, East Finchley, London, N2 9ED, United Kingdom
Str. Armeneasca 28/1, office 1, Chisinau MD-2012, Republic of Moldova, Europe
Printed at: see last page
ISBN: 978-620-7-61070-9

Contents

Presentation

In your essence , models mathematicians they are as maps simplified reality , created with the aim of understanding and solving real - world complexities . These models find application in one myriad of contexts , covering from the management of production lines in companies to organization of postal services , resource planning in public institutions , construction of hydroelectric plants and development of vehicle engines . Here goes lots of things . Essentially , the models mathematicians permeate all you aspects of life modern , serving as crucial tools for understanding scenarios and finding solutions efficient to achieve goals specific . This principle extends even The sphere of nutrition , both of beings humans as well as other beings alive .

Since the middle of the 20th century , professionals from different areas began The employ methods mathematicians to face challenges related to food management , emerging So the classic problem called diet to feed . These challenges are not limited just to the cost and benefits of food , but also encompass the achievement of objectives nutritional smart . To address effectively the issue of diet food , first is necessary understand the nature of the problem in yes . When planning The someone 's food , including one's own, arise several questions : how much food will be used , the cost involved , the nutrients essentials , the number of consumers to be fed , the calories to be consumed , the foods that don't provoke allergies and the ideal meal frequency to maintain good health . These questions , which constitute the core of the diet problem food , can be addressed and resolved through optimization mathematics .

This book aims to present the history of the diet problem food , or in the scene modern Brazilian and, mainly , the methods mathematicians known and robust in the academic area . Simple model descriptions , such as linear optimization , even algorithms evolutionists who work in this feeding scenario , are presented in this book to facilitate study and curiosity about This one problem specific what happens in large organizational environments public and private to problem environments trivialities of people 's daily lives .

In addition to this presentation initial , present book contains three chapters . The first addresses the scenario current society Brazilian and the vision statistics of the diet problem to feed . Afterwards , the second chapter describe you methods mathematicians and advances in diet programming food . Finally , the third chapter dedicates himself to master 's study in diet problem scenario food , applying one bimobile strategy , with analysis experimental , including case studies simulated , with different quantities of decision variables , accompanied by the results experimental .

## Chapter 1

Lifestyle in society and its problem to feed

In this first chapter , we explore a historical overview of the issues food faced by the population Brazilian , covering the period since mid- twentieth century , where had the beginning of concern about health feed , until the second decade of the 21st century . Here, the questions food they are examined on a spectrum more broad , including both the insecurity to feed As for obesity , the latter is a reflection of consumption excessive food .

These solutions quantitative allow one approach more structured and objective at decision - making per part of organizations public and private . When applying methods statistics and mathematics , the chapter illustrates as you challenges food can be understood and addressed in a more effective , with strategies based in data and analysis accurate .

1.1 Problem feed not Brazil

He was only at 1940s that the Brazil began to recognize officially The existence of hunger among its population . This landmark occurred with the publication of the book "The Geography of Hunger " (1946) by Josue de Castro. In this seminal work , Castro created the first map of hunger in Brazil , detailing you habits food regional (Castro, 1984; Vasconcelos, 2008; Sa, 2011). Previous to this study , the perception of hunger in the country was fragmented and not existed researches comprehensive evidence that showed The insecurity feed among Brazilians . Through your research , Castro revealed the seriousness of the insecurity food , highlighting that the majority of the population consumed any less calories than Minimum necessary . An example emblematic he was your study about families workers in Recife, Pernambuco, whose diet daily , composed mainly per Sugar , coffee, beef jerky , flour, beans and bread, added up around 1645 calories - below the minimum threshold of 2000 calories recommended for health food (Castro, 1984; MS, 2004; ANVISA, 2005; Vasconcelos, 2008). Castro 's publications opened path to futures studies about hunger in Brazil .

Since 1975, the Brazilian Institute of Geography and Statistics (IBGE) has conducted censuses on The insecurity food in Brazil . A insecurity to feed refers to insufficient availability and access physical , social and financial to food , increasing the risk of hunger . In the first years of these surveys , IBGE identified that more than half of the population faced insecurity to feed . However , from the 21st century onwards , there was a reduction in this frame , in part due to the process of industrialization and urbanization of the country . These phenomena had impacts positive at quality of life and diversification of the food supply , both natural and how much industrialized . Furthermore , policies government , allies The expansion technological and industrial, contributed to reducing you security problems food (IBGE, 2021).

However , as the insecurity to feed decreased , there was an increase at incidence of obesity in all tracks age groups and social classes , configuring itself as a new public health challenge - a phenomenon also observed globally (WHO, 2021). Records indicate that, in 1980s , around 18% of Brazilians they were obese . In the decades following periods , this percentage increased significantly . For example , in 2018, half of the population he was above ideal weight, while 35% still faced insecurity to feed . A evolution of these health issues related to food can be viewed at Figure 1, where data on insecurity food and obesity they were grouped under the ' Problem ' category Food ' (IBGE, 2021).

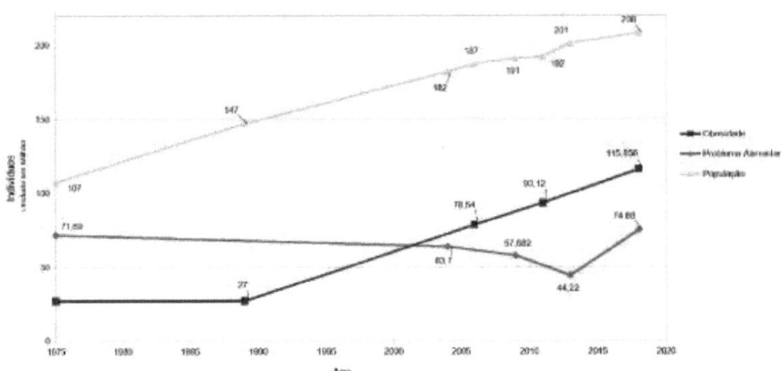

Source: IBGE; Ministry of Health. Own preparation .
Figure 1. History of Obesity , Problem Food and Population Growth between 1975 and 2018, in Brazil .

Face you challenges of malnutrition and obesity , both problems food critics , requires strategies effective . A central approach and promoting food consumption no just accessible , but also healthy . That can be achieved through diets balanced , developed per specialists , adapted to the needs individual or groups with characteristics metabolism and habits food similar .

In Brazil , the increase at prevalence of obesity and a concern for the body , and re-education to feed he has intensified demand per professionals specialized in nutrition . Between 2003 and 2013, there was an increase of approximately 200% in the number of nutritionists registered us Family Health Support Centers (NASF) by municipality , jumping from 123 to 340 teams. In 2019, the country registered more than 132 thousand professionals acting in the area (Vasconcelos, Sousa, 2015; Sydow, 2021). However , adopting and maintaining one diet healthy and a challenge constant and individual, which requires adaptations to the throughout life . This is due to metabolic variances the body 's natural and unavoidable changes in habits that impact demand per calories and nutrients , as well as others needs physiological (Cederholm et al., 2017).

Same individuals with clear health goals can to develop bad habits food . That occurs , in part , because the brain is not always able to reliably assess the cost - benefit associate to the food consumption . Furthermore , decision making involves scenarios complexes with multiple variables interconnected (Evert et al., 2019). Therefore , the intervention of nutritionists and education to feed continued they are crucial to guide choices healthy and sustainable , both at the individual and collective
.

The technology also grown up us latest years . They exist several health services , tools and applications that offer support and control of diet and exercise to the users . These services offer guides food , created per through optimization methods to help

4

you users to follow diets healthy : applications as *MyFitnessPal* [1], *sites like Perfectbody me* [2] and programs as *NutriGenie* [3]. These are examples that the proposition and synthesis of recommendation systems personalized , aimed at diets food , are viable .

Both health professionals regarding tools and services related The feeding often resort to concepts and methods settled down at literature that addresses you nutrition challenges . In particular, technologies digital data that provide information vital - like guides food , monitoring nutrient consumption and diets personalized - are you results of studies and applications mathematics good substantiated . Many of these advances technological employ one variety of methods , including approaches combinatorial , multi-objective and programming linear and non-linear , which has your roots in the first pregnancy problem food , widely explored since mid 20th century .

These tools are deep integrated into society Brazilian , whether us medical offices , whether us applications furniture used per individuals in your daily . Although these technologies approach one gamma variety of questions specific health issues , all they share a common basis in the classic problem of nutrition : the diet to feed . This core common underline The continued importance of diet to feed as a fundamental pillar in health and well-being .

1.2 Diet problem to feed at perspective statistic

Concern about a feeding proper can be translated mathematically in a diet problem . This approach mathematics focuses at amount adequate amount of nutrients and micronutrients to be consumed . Diets , in this context , has goals smart , like weight loss or health maintenance , and should cater to various restrict . A diet that doesn't fulfills these restricted and considered ineffective , failing in meet the needs individual 's diet . Thus, the formulation of problems dietary employment programming techniques math to find solutions viable solutions that optimize an objective single or balance multiple goals conflicting .

The first mathematical formulations of problems dietary for humans emerged at half of the 20th century , during events such as World War II and the Cold War. The armed forms of the United States sought ways to feed soldiers minimizing costs and maximizing The efficiency (Dooren, 2018; Barbosa, 2014). Pioneers in this field were the economist George Stigler and the mathematician George Dantzig. Stigler and Dantzig applied Linear Programming models to achieve these objectives .

George Stigler proposed one solution approximate for the demand of the exercise North American. He formulated one 39 dollar diet with 77 types of foods different , respecting the 9 nutrients essentials for a man adult . This diet included items such as wheat flour, milk evaporated , cabbage , spinach and dried beans (MIT, 2023). George Dantzig, by your time , improved that approach after developing the Simplex algorithm in 1947, finding one solute great for the problem proposed (Dooren, 2018;

---

[1] The *MyFitnessPal,* Inc service records the user 's meals and diets , in addition to making weight loss goals . (MYFITNESSPAL, 2024).
[2] Service that creates a meal plan according to the user 's answers to a questionnaire , in addition to recording the user 's consumption (UAB, 2024).
[3] Software developed for the group of researchers at Stanford University , offers a nutrition program (NUTRIGENIE , 2024).

Barbosa, 2014; Gass & Harris, 2001).

In addition to your use in context military , Linear Programming also became a valuable tool at formulation of animal feed in the agribusiness sector (Sklan & Dariel , 1992; Gass & Harris, 2001) .

You first studies in programming dietetics opened path to a exploration deeper in this field. New dimensions of the problem they were introduced , encompassing sustainability , productivity and health (Amin, Gow-Mulligan, Guoqing , 2019). Subsequently , formulate further complex and technical advanced resolution they were proposals , marking a step forward significant in the area (Santos, Sichieri , Darmon et al., 2018; Vieux, Maillot, Drewnowski, 2019). Among the various techniques , programming linear mathematics continues to be the most employed (Dooren, 2018; Patil, Kasturi, 2016; Sklan , Dariel, 1992).

However , the literature specialized reveals one plurality of initiatives to formulate and solve the problem of diet to the over the last few decades (Dooren, 2018). The variety of design decisions involved generates many different approaches and formulas, which can complicate making comparisons systematic between them . In view of this , it is pertinent accomplish one summary of practices more known at resolute of that classic problem . This synthesis he must consider also you advances technological recent ones that provided new solution methodologies . At the same time , these innovations he comes being applied at society , highlighting the relevance practice and continue studying the diet to feed

Chapter 2

Optimization mathematics as troubleshooting

This chapter explores the main approaches and methodologies mathematics that are widely discussed and applied at literature academic related to the diet problem to feed . While it 's not possible include all you methods existing in the vast universe academic , the focus relapse about the techniques more recognized .

The discussion starts with classic models , some of which they were adopted and implemented for the economist George Stigler and mathematician George Dantzig. Advancing in addition of these fundamentals , explore models innovative joints in artificial intelligence , such as algorithms evolutionary . These models allow the construction of scenarios more complexes and the inclusion of variables additional factors that influence indirectly at food healthy . The goal of this chapter and provide one understanding comprehensive approach mathematics used to solve problems as This is the classic problem presented at half of the 20th century .

2.1 Programming diet math to feed

When we face problems that contain elements quantitative and require The choose the best option among several alternatives , modeling mathematics becomes an essential tool . The Optimization Mathematics , too known as Programming Mathematics , and the process that seeks find the best solutions to such problems .

The problem with diet food is a classic example of an optimization problem mathematics . In it, the goal is to identify the ideal diet , taking in consideration several elements quantitative and pre- defined criteria . A method widely used at resolution of these problems , and that still keeps your relevance at literature , and Linear Programming .

Linear Programming is a robust technique that applies to a vast range of optimization problems at decision - making . Its usefulness go beyond planning dietary human , covering also questions how the production in factories , storage and transport in distributors , minimizing costs in power generation in hydroelectric plants , and even decisions to purchase products and services . All these scenarios can be efficiently managed through the programming application mathematics (Raimundo, 2014; Barbosa, 2014).

Its formulation simplest consists at search for the best resource distribution able to meet one linear objective function and restrictions linear , conducting to a linear programming problem (Sklan ; Dariel, 1992) (Barbosa, 2014) . In a description fast , linear programming requires three components (Patil; Kasturi, 2016) (Sklan ; Dariel, 1992):

- Decision variables , associated to the resources used in the problem ;
- objective function , which expresses mathematically what you want to see gift at solution excellent ;
- Restrictions or contour leads involved , generally described in the form of equations and inequalities linear .

As an example definition illustration of these three elements , considering a problem diet fiction food , we have :

- Which foods (among a universe of foods available for selection) must be consumed , with each food he has your cost associate and its composition specification nutritional (information these available a priori).

- As objective functions , one can consider simultaneously maximize following a pattern of distribution of energy and quantity of food to the throughout meals and minimize the total cost of acquisition and preparation .
- What calories and nutrients (fiber , protein , vitamins and salts) minerals) are necessary for consumption human aiming to meet restrictions daily (for example , values minimum and/ or maximum).

To ride This one model per means of equations , it is necessary define the decision variables , formulate the objective function and, therefore , Finally , include the restrictions . It is necessary to formulate a equation for each restriction found in the problem , that is, it must build , for example , two restriction equations with all decision variables if the problem inform that there are two restrictions that all variables must to respect . In a representation mathematics , the model general diet problem to feed in linear programming we have :

- Food Quantity Vector , represented per X of size n, where is x_i the quantity of food $i, x_i \subset Z_+$ e $1 \leq i \leq n$;
- Food Cost Vector, represented per C of size n, where c . and the real unit cost of the food $i, c_i \subset R_+$ e $1 \leq i \leq n$;

- Nutrient Matrix associates to the food , represented per size $R\ mxn$, what is r_{ji} the real value of the nutrient j in food $i, r_{ji} \subset R_+, 1 \leq j \leq m$ e $1 \leq i \leq n$;
- Nutrient Restrictions Vector , represented per B of size m, where b . and the real value of $j, b_j \subset R_+$ e $1 \leq j \leq m$; nutrient restriction

Minimize the objective function :

$$min_x f(x) = c_1 x_1 + c_2 x_2 + ... + c_n x_n \qquad (1)$$

where c_n it's cost per nth unit food , subject to:

$$r_{11} x_1 + r_{12} x_2 + r_{13} x_3 + ... + r_{1n} x_n \geq b_1 (Restrição\ 1),$$

$$r_{21} x_1 + r_{22} x_2 + r_{23} x_3 + ... + r_{2n} x_n \geq b_2 (Restrição\ 2),$$

$$r_{31} x_1 + r_{32} x_2 + r_{33} x_3 + ... + r_{3n} x_n \geq b_3 (Restrição\ 3),$$

$$...$$

$$r_{m1} x_1 + r_{m2} x_2 + r_{m3} x_3 + ... + r_{mn} x_n \geq b_m (Restrição\ m), \qquad (2)$$

ro value being restriction unit m do n - th food . mn

Linear programming will in search for solutions doable great . The solution he must indicate which foods will be consumed and in what quantity , to meet the need for a person . Same no being the case of the formulation above , it is worth highlighting that Linear Programming is a methodology that can to contain several strategies mathematics . They exist cases in uses value variables binaries and integers , such as Mixed Integer Linear Programming . In order to resolve programming problems mathematics that require the use of variables whole , one approach mixed can be adopted , combining simplex and the search method in tree denominated *Branch-and-Bound* . This approach mixed and often complemented per domain reduction techniques based in restriction programming or generation automatic cuts. These improvements reduce the scope of the search and improve considerably the performance of the solution algorithm . All these extensions they are at the moment included us main *solvers* in the area of linear programming (Santos; Sichieri ; Darmon et al., 2018) (Dooren, 2018) (Patil; Kasturi, 2016) (Sklan ; Dariel, 1992) (Vieux, Maillot, Drewnowski, 2019).

An example of a real case was the study by Amol Nayakappa Patil and Sidharth Kasturi, from 2016, in which authors used linear programming to investigate the problem of deciding the diet of human beings between 40 and 45 years old with the aim of reducing the costs of the diet to be constructed . With a set of eight food and seven nutrients , the authors formulated one diet with cost monetary value 43.5. Furthermore , they believe that the use of this method can be applied also problems related The resource allocation optimization in health.

An example remarkable at literature and the study of Quenia Dos Santos and collaborators in 2018, which adopted linear programming to develop one diet optimized . The study included sixty - eight food and sought minimize the difference in relation to intake observed average diet at population Brazilian . The main objective was to identify choices food ideals that fulfilled the recommendations nutrition to reduce The intake inadequate nutrients . Although you authors initially no have found solutions faUable , resorted to methods of relaxing restrictions , allowing the model adjust you limits of restrictions to obtain results more aligned with expectations . This approach resulted in one diet able to avoid The inadequacy of more than 60% of nutrients at sample populational studied .

In literature , also they are found extensions that incorporate objective functions and/ or restrictions non-linear in diet applications food (Jardim et al., 2013; Barre, Perignon, 2018). A application of functions non-linear transform the problem in one programming question not linear.

As for solver tools, there is a variety both in terms of commercial as well as free-code . The trading tools tend to be more efficient , but Free - code *solvers* too they are able to solve problems mathematicians complex and are widely used in the medium academic . Examples of *solvers* Commercial programs that work with linear and non -linear programming include MATLAB with Simulink and Gurobi , while IBM's CPLEX is focused in linear programming . In the open -code spectrum , AMPL and SCIP handle both scenarios mathematics , and GNU's COIN-OR Foundation and GLPK tools are specialized in linear programming . Although AMPL is open source with a license commercial , this available free of charge for academic purposes no commercials , so like other commercial solvers that offer licenses academics free (Gearhart, Adair, 2013).

2.1.1 Diet examples to feed

Two examples of the use of linear programming in the diet problem they are gifts in this section with the aim of familiarizing solver tools and linear programming in code . The first problem use the commercial tool Gurobi is already the second problem uses the open-source AMPL tool.

Problem 1

This diet problem to feed it is gift at collection of examples of the Gurobi [4]tool . The programming language of this problem and Python, however This tool supports too much languages known .

Have the nine information foods with four nutrients and prices unitaries . You want to create one possible diet daily with the minor cost possible of these foods available at Table 1. It is known that the cost of this diet It is strongly related to the amount of food and it is not enough to just get the food more cheap to create the diet , you need also to meet you nutrient requirements in order to have consumption healthy to the human being . In this way, in Table 2 has information about how much acceptable he can consume you nutrients necessary .

	Hamburger	Chicken	Hot dog	Potato Fries	Macaron	Pizza	Salad	Milk	Ice cream
Calories	410	420	560	380	320	320	320	100	330
Protein	24	32	20	4	12	15	31	8	8
Fat	26	10	32	19	10	12	12	2.5	10
Sodium	730	1190	1800	270	930	820	1230	125	180
Price	2.49	2.89	1.50	1.89	2.09	1.99	2.49	0.89	1.59

Source: Own elaboration ..

Table 1. Food and Nutrient Table for Problem 1.

Nutrient	Minimum	Maximum
Calories	100	2200
Protein	91	100000*
Fat	0	65
Sodium	0	1779
* The maximum value of Protein is infinite , not has a precise value found .		

Source: Own elaboration ..

Table 2. Nutrient Intake Table for Problem 1 .

noticed that and possible elaborate you three programming components mathematics . The objective function of this problem and minimize the cost of this diet ; the decision variables are the quantities and prices of food gift at Table 1; and the constraints of the problems they are you nutrient consumption intervals gift at Table 2. How there is a maximum and minimum for each nutrient restriction , it is necessary produce two restriction equations of the same nutrient in order to work on the range allowed . Modeling mathematically , we have :

- Food Quantity Vector , represented per x in size 9 , in which x_i é the amount of food i, $x_i \subset Z_+$ e $1 \leq i \leq 9$;

- Food Cost Vector , represented per c in size 9 , in which c. and the real unit cost of the food i, $c_i \subset R_+$ e $1 \leq i \leq 9$;

- Nutrient Matrix associates to the food , represented per r in size 4 x 9 , where is r_{ji} the real value of the nutrient j in food i, $r_{ji} \subset R_+$, $1 \leq j \leq 4$ e $1 \leq i \leq 9$;

- Nutrient Restrictions Matrix , represented per b in size 4x2 with the values minimum and

---

[4]The example it is available on the official Gurobi website , at : < https://www.gurobi.com/documentation/10.0/examples/diet py.html >.

maximum , where is b_{jk} the real value of nutrient restriction j from the break limit k, $b_{jk} \subset R_+$, $1 \leq j \leq 4$ e $1 \leq k \leq 2$;

Funpao Goal :

$$min_x f(x) = \quad c_1 x_1 + c_2 x_2 + \ldots + c_9 x_9 = \sum_{i=1}^{9} c_i x_i \qquad (3)$$

, subject to:

$$r_{11} x_1 + r_{12} x_2 + r_{13} x_3 + \ldots + r_{19} x_9 \geq b_{11} (Restrição\ 1\ mínima),$$

$$r_{11} x_1 + r_{12} x_2 + r_{13} x_3 + \ldots + r_{19} x_9 \leq b_{12} (Restrição\ 1\ máxima),$$

$$r_{21} x_1 + r_{22} x_2 + r_{23} x_3 + \ldots + r_{29} x_9 \geq b_{21} (Restrição\ 2\ mínima),$$

$$r_{21} x_1 + r_{22} x_2 + r_{23} x_3 + \ldots + r_{29} x_9 \leq b_{22} (Restrição\ 2\ máxima),$$

$$\ldots$$

$$r_{41} x_1 + r_{42} x_2 + r_{43} x_3 + \ldots + r_{49} x_9 \geq b_{41} (Restrição\ 4\ mínima),$$

$$r_{41} x_1 + r_{42} x_2 + r_{43} x_3 + \ldots + r_{49} x_9 \leq b_{42} (Restrição\ 4\ máxima) \qquad (4)$$

Is it possible to convert this model for the Python programming language - with the Gurobi tool . However , as This tool has rules that limit the free construction of modeling you problems , certain element definitions must be changed , for example converting vector variables and matrices to Python dictionaries . Realizing it is talk , we have the code of this model (Code 1). The code below describe you steps for defining variables and functions necessary to build This one problem . It should be noted that you need have the gurobi library and python present on the computer case want replicate the problem . This code can be built in a file *diet.py and* run in the terminal.

```
# import the tool import                 # model
gurobipy as gp from gurobipy             model = gp.Model ("diet")
import GRB                               # Define who are the decision variables , which are
# must be placed put the                 you food (food), which and written as :
information needed in dictionaries       var = model.addVars (food, name=" buy ")
categories , minNutri , maxNutri =       # defines the objective function of the problem ,
gp.multidict ({                          which is minimize cost .
' calories ': [1800, 2200],              # objective function is a sum- product of food and
' protein ': [91, GRB.INFINITY], '       costs. Instead of writing the function whole , we can
fat ':   [0, 65],                        to write :
'sodium': [0, 1779 ] } )                 model.setObjective (sum(var[c]* cost [c] for c in
# creates the nail dictionary from       food), GRB.MINIMIZE)
the tool itself                          # define also as you will restrict your com limits of
food, cost = gp.multidict ({             min e max por um looping: for cat in categories :
'hamburger': 2.49, ' chicken ':          model.addRange (sum( valueNutri [c, cat] * var[c]
2.89, ' hotdog ': 1.50, ' fries ':       for c in food), minNutri [cat], maxNutri [cat], cat)
    1.89,                                # to solve the problem model.optimize ()
'macaroni': 2.09, 'pizza':     1.99,     # method of presenting the solution def
```

' salad ':	2.49,	printSolution ( ):

<table>
<tr><td>

```
' salad ':        2.49,
' milk ':         0.89,
' ice cream ': 1.59 } )
#    creates a normal dictionary of
nutrients for each food , where the
key is a food and nutrient tuple .
valueNutri = {
('hamburger', calories ): 410,
('hamburger', ' protein '): 24,
```

</td><td>

```
printSolution ( ):
if  model.status  ==  GRB.OPTIMAL:  print('\ nCost :
%g' % model.ObjVal )
```

</td></tr>
<tr><td>

```
('hamburger', ' fat '): 26,
('hamburger', 'sodium'): 730,
# repeat for everyone you foods ...
(' ice cream ', ' calories '): 330,
(' ice cream ', ' protein '): 8,
(' ice cream ', ' fat '): 10,
(' ice cream ', 'sodium'): 180}
```

</td><td>

```
print('\ nVariables :')
for c in food:
if var[c].X > 0.0001:
print( '%s %g' % (c, var[c].X))
else:
print( 'No solution ')
printSolution ( )
```

</td></tr>
</table>

Source: Gurobi

Code 1 : Problem Code 1 using Gurobi .

Problem 2

This diet problem to feed it is gift at collection of examples of the AMPL 5 tool . The programming language of this problem is its own, however This tool supports too much languages known . Have the eight information foods with four types of vitamins , which are you nutrients , and prices unitaries . You want to create one possible diet with the smallest cost possible of these foods available , present at Table 3 , with the requirement Minimum consumption diary be 700% for each nutrient .

	Beef	Chicken	Fish	Ham	Macaroni and Cheese	Roll of Meat	Spaghetti and	Peru
A (%)	60	8	8	40	15	70	25	60
W (%)	20	0	10	40	35	30	50	20
B1 (%)	10	20	15	35	15	15	25	15
B2 (%)	15	20	10	10	15	15	15	10
Price	3.19	2.59	2.59	2.89	1.89	1.99	1.99	2.49

Source: Own elaboration .

Table 3. Food and Nutrient Table for Problem 2.

5   There are other problems available on the official AMPL website , for more details of this example access in :
< https://ampl.com/wp-content/uploads/Chapter-2-Diet-and-Other-Input-Models-Minimizing-Costs-AMP L-Book.pdf >.

observed that the problem want ramp up one diet that minimizes the costs of these food and quantity of food he must contain the percentage value of nutrients bigger or equal to 700%. Modeling mathematically , we have :

- Food Quantity Vector , represented per x in size 8 , where . x_i ' and the amount of food $i, x_i \subset Z_+$ e 8;

- Food Cost Vector , represented per c in size 8 , where is c_i the real unit cost of the food $i, c_i \subset R_+$ e $1 \leq i \leq 8$;

- Nutrient Matrix associates to the food, represented per r in size 4 x 8, where is r_{ji} the real value of the nutrient j in food i, $r_{ji} \subset R_+$, $1 \leq j \leq 4$ e $1 \leq i \leq 8$;

- Nutrient Restrictions Vector, represented per b in size 4, where is b_j the real value of the nutrient restriction j, $b_j \subset R_+$, $1 \leq j \leq 4$;

Function Goal :

$$\min_x f(x) = c_1 x_1 + c_2 x_2 + \dots + c_8 x_8 = \sum_{i=1}^{8} c_i x_i \qquad (5)$$

, subject to

$$r_{11} x_1 + r_{12} x_2 + r_{13} x_3 + \dots + r_{18} x_8 \geq b_1 \ (Restrição\ 1),$$

$$r_{21} x_1 + r_{22} x_2 + r_{23} x_3 + \dots + r_{28} x_8 \geq b_2 \ (Restrição\ 2),$$

$$r_{31} x_1 + r_{32} x_2 + r_{33} x_3 + \dots + r_{38} x_8 \geq b_3 \ (Restrição\ 3),$$

$$r_{41} x_1 + r_{42} x_2 + r_{43} x_3 + \dots + r_{48} x_8 \geq b_4 \ (Restrição\ 4) \qquad (6)$$

Respecting the rules of the AMPL tool, it is possible to convert this problem for language computational , having the code of this model in Code 2. To replicate the problem , you must contain the AMPL tool on the computer . This code can be built in a file called *diet2.mod* is executed in the AMPL terminal, present Code 3.

```
# defines the decision variables
var steak >= 0; var chicken >= 0;
var fish >= 0; var ham >= 0;
var macaroni >= 0; var MeatRoll >=0;
var spaghetti >= 0; var turkey >= 0;
# defines the objective function minimize cost :
3.19* steak + 2.59* chicken + 2.29* chicken + 2.89* ham + 1.89* macaroni + 1.99* beef roll + 1.99* spaghetti + 2.49* turkey ;
# define restrictions
subject to A:
60* steak + 8* chicken + 8* chicken + 40* ham + 15* macaroni + 70* beef roll + 25* spaghetti + 60* turkey >= 700;

subject to C:
20* steak + 0* chicken + 10* chicken + 40* ham + 35* macaroni + 30* meat roll + 50* spaghetti + 20* turkey >= 700;
subject to B1:
10* steak + 20* chicken + 15* chicken + 35* ham + 15* macaroni + 15* beef roll + 25* spaghetti + 10* turkey >= 700;
subject to B2:
15* steak + 20* chicken + 10* chicken + 10* ham + 15* macaroni + 15* beef roll + 15* spaghetti + 15* turkey >= 700;
```

Source: Own elaboration .

Code 2. Code for Problem 2 using AMPL.

```
ampl : model diet2.mod;
ampl : solve;
MINOS 5.5: optimal solution found.
6    iterations, objective 88.2
ampl : display steak , chicken , fish , ham , macaroni, beef roll , spaghetti , turkey ; steak = 0
franc = 0
fish = 0
```

```
ham = 0
macaroni = 46.6667
rollMeat = -3.69159e-18
spaghetti = -4.05347e-16
turkey = 0
```


Code 3. Presentation of results with AMPL.

2.2 Optimization multi objective mathematics

Although not always be explicitly recognized , most optimization problems of practical interest involves the consideration of multiple goals . An observation attentive to decisions everyday reveals that often we face situations with objectives conflicting . Examples common include search per high- end products nail quality low , the choosing a transport service that is to the at the same time accessible and fast , or carrying out a task in the shortest possible time without compromise quality . In these situations , the goals they are lots of times inversely proportional , leading to the need for a balance where you results be great for both you goals . This type of dilemma is characteristic of multi- objective optimization problems , which can be addressed through multi - objective programming .

When an optimization problem involves just one objective function or one linear combination of multiples fungdes-objective , it is classified as a single - objective optimization problem . In contrast , problems that incorporate multiple funQdes-objective in conflict they are acquaintances as optimization problems multi-objective (Carvalho, 2014; Coello, 2006; Veldhuizen, 1999).

In the context of multi- objective problems with objectives conflicting , no exist one better solution that optimizes all you goals simultaneously . Instead Furthermore , there are solutions great . Mapping the problem within the limits of the objectives , we observed that the solutions great tend to form a pattern known as Pareto frontier . Solutions next The it is border they are considered great or non-dominated , while those far from the border tend to offer results lower . Therefore , solutions outside the Pareto Frontier are considered inefficient or dominated per for the any less one Pareto- optimal solution (Mendes, 2013; Carvalho, 2014).

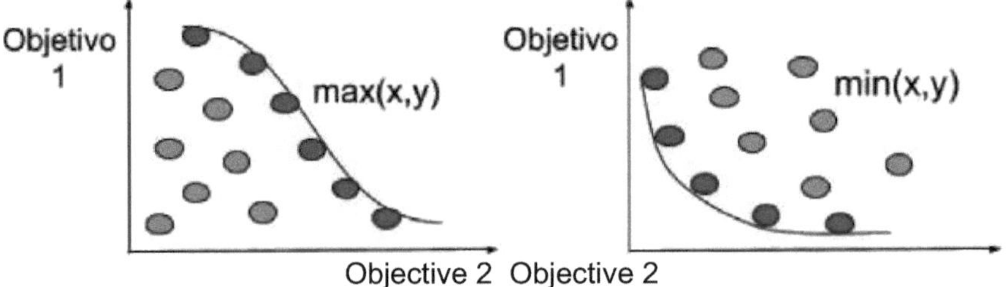

Figure 2. Examples of Pareto frontier , showing solutions dominated (in gray) and non-dominated (in red), for scenarios of maximizing and minimizing objectives

In summary , a Pareto- optimal solution defined by the condition where it 's not possible improve performance on a goal without simultaneously compromise to the at least one other goal involved (Ferreira, 2017; Zhenkui & Zhen, 2009; Mendes, 2013;

Carvalho, 2014). This concept is illustrated at Figure 2, which presents two examples distinct from the Pareto frontier . In the first example (a left), we observe the maximization of two objectives , while in the second (on the right), the minimization of two objectives and portrayed . You points marked in red represent the solutions great or Pareto- optimal , located at border demarcated by the continuous curve. Already the points in gray they are solutions that are dominated per for the any less one Pareto - optimal solution , indicating inferior performance in comparison with solutions great .

Return to diet scenario food to create a scenario fiction of a diet problem food in order to familiarize as can be worked in this multi- objective scenario . You want a diet strict in which it should worry about hundreds of nutrients food . The first objective and minimize the amount of nutrient unwanted , for example cholesterol . The second objective is to minimize the total cost of construction of this diet . Modeling mathematically This one problem , we have these elements :

- Size X Food Vector n in what $x_i \subset X, 1 \le i \le n,$ and the quantity i - th unitary food ;

- Size C Cost Vector n what is $: c_i \subset C, 1 \le i \le n,$ the cost per unit (including preparation time) of the i -th food ;

- Cholesterol Nutrient Vector S of size n, at what $s_i \subset R, 1 \le i \le n$ é o value per i - th cholesterol unit food .

- Nutrient Matrix R without Size cholesterol mxn , where , $r_{ji} \subset R,$ $1 \le j \le m$ e $1 \le i \le n,$ and the value per j - th unit i - th nutrient food ;

• Constraint Vector B to *stop* size m where , $b_j \subset B, 1 \le j \le m,$ and the value of the i -th restriction .

The construction of the model multi-objective he has you same components of a mono- objective model (decision variables , objective function and restrictions). Furthermore , the objective functions must to respect all constraints in order to find solutions great . Finally , a problem multi-objective Hiccup in the context of diet to feed can then be formulated as follows:

Define the following objective functions :

$$Min\, F_1: \quad f_1(x) = c_1 x_1 + c_2 x_2 + c_3 x_3 + ... + c_n x_n \tag{7}$$

$$Min\, F_2: \quad f_2(x) = s_1 x_1 + s_2 x_2 + s_3 x_3 + ... + s_n x_n \tag{8}$$

where $c_n^{\,(}$ is the cost per n -th unit decision variable of the objective function and x_n the objective function is f_1 e s_n é the value of s - th cholesterol objective function $x_n^{\,(}$ decision variable subject to $'f_2'$:

$$s_{11}x_1 + s_{12}x_2 + s_{13}x_3 + ... + s_{1n}x_n \leq b_1 \quad \text{(Restrição 1)}$$

$$s_{21}x_1 + s_{22}x_2 + s_{23}x_3 + ... + s_{2n}x_n \leq b_2 \quad \text{(Restrição 2)}$$

$$...$$

$$s_{m1}x_1 + s_{m2}x_2 + s_{m3}x_3 + ... + s_{mn}x_n \leq b_m \quad \text{(Restrição m)} \tag{10}$$

where s_{mn} and the cost per unit of n - th decision variable x_n.

This model is an example general way of modeling a problem that contains the multi-objective characteristic . It may exist cases what is your work more than two objective functions and other cases that employ both maximize functions how much minimize functions you goals . When working with multi- objective problems , you are concerned with visualize the Pareto Frontier to understand the behavior of solutions and find solutions great .

Furthermore , when dealing with multi - objective problems , many times and advantageous transform these problems in mono- objective problems . This transformation allows techniques optimization pattern can be applied without modifications extensive . To perform that transformation , are applied methods they seek preserve the characteristics essential objectives originals . One of the classic methods is the Weights Method . In this method , each objective and multiplied by a smart weight and, in then all you goals weighted they are added together to form a single goal . Selection of different weights he can lead to solutions different , and this technique can be used to explore the solution space possible .

Another method known and the Method Hierarchical , too known as approach lexicography , and a technique that addresses that challenge Prioritizing you goals . One of the objectives is optimized first , while the other objectives they are treaties as restrictions . Once optimized the first objective , the next and optimized considering the solution optimum of the previous objective , and thus per against . Unfortunately , it is a method that does not explore completely the Pareto set, which is the set of solutions great in a multi- objective sense .

Many different problems and contexts they can demand or benefit more of one method than another. Therefore , it is crucial to choose the right technique more appropriate according to the nature of the problem and the requirements specific to the decision process .

In the same way that there are digital tools for Single- Objective Optimization , there are private and open-source tools for multi- objective optimization . For private tools , Gurobi and CPLEX offer resources for solving multi - objective problems . As for the open-source side , many languages they are focused on the Python programming language , as it is popularly used for problems mathematicians . The Pulp library and the DESDEO tool (Misitano ; Saini, 2021) offer many multi - objective optimization methods in this language . Therefore, it requires a little programming knowledge to use the tools .

Recently , the algorithms multi- objective evolutionary he has won emphasis at problem approach multi-objective , given its efficiency in meet solutions optimized for multiple criteria simultaneously . In comparison with methods traditional , the use of algorithms evolutionary offers one approach adaptable to the problems when is it desirable to explore one wide range of solutions possible .

2.2.1 Example of a multi- objective model

An example of using multi - objective linear programming in the diet problem it is gift in this section with the aim of familiarizing solver tools and linear programming in code . An example uses the Python programming language with the Pulp library .

Problem 1

We return to the first problem introduced under the title " *Optimization Mathematics as troubleshooting* " . This problem he does part of the collection of examples made available by the Gurobi tool . Imagine a diet whose goal it is simultaneously reduce calorie consumption and increase The protein intake according to foods gifts at Table 1. Restrictions detailed at Table 2 must be observed , considering these two objectives that may be conflicting . One approach to solving this complexity and employ the Weights Method .

Modeling mathematically , we have :

- Food Quantity Vector , represented per x in size 9 , where . x_i and the amount of food i, $x_i \subset Z_+$ e $1 \le i \le 9$;

- Food Calories Vector , represented per c in size 9 , where is ca_i the real unit cost of the food i, $ca_i \subset R_+$ e $1 \le i \le 9$;

- Protein Calories Vector , represented per c in size 9 , where is $p_i{}'$ the real unit cost of the food i, $p_i \subset R_+$ e $1 \le i \le 9$; ;

- Nutrient Matrix associates to the food , represented per r in size 4 x 9 , where is r_{ji} the real value of the nutrient j in food i, $r_{ji} \subset R_+$, $1 \le j \le 4$ e $1 \le i \le 9$;
- Nutrient Restrictions Matrix , represented per b in size 4x2 with the values minimum and maximum , where is b_{jk} the real value of the nutrient restriction j from the break limit k, k, $b_{jk} \subset R_+$, $1 \le j \le 4$ e $1 \le k \le 2$;

- *weight1* and *weight2* they are values positive real constants (Я +) of weights for the function objective of minimizing the amount of calories and maximizing the amount of protein , respectively . Furthermore , $peso_1 + peso_2 = 1.0$

Functions Goals :

$$\text{Calorias: } \min_x f_1(x) = ca_1 x_1 + ca_2 x_2 + \ldots + ca_9 x_9 = \sum_{i=1}^{9} ca_i x_i \qquad (11)$$

$$\text{Proteinas: } \max_x f_2(x) = p_1 x_1 + p_2 x_2 + \ldots + p_9 x_9 = \sum_{i=1}^{9} p_i x_i \qquad (12)$$

$$\min_x F(x) = (f_1(x),\ f_2(x)) = peso_1 \sum_{i=1}^{9} ca_i x_i - peso_2 \sum_{i=1}^{9} p_i x_i \qquad (13)$$

, subject to:

$$r_{11}x_1 + r_{12}x_2 + r_{13}x_3 + \ldots + r_{19}x_9 \geq b_{11}\,(Restrição\ 1\ mínima),$$

$$r_{11}x_1 + r_{12}x_2 + r_{13}x_3 + \ldots + r_{19}x_9 \leq b_{12}\,(Restrição\ 1\ máxima),$$

$$r_{21}x_1 + r_{22}x_2 + r_{23}x_3 + \ldots + r_{29}x_9 \geq b_{21}\,(Restrição\ 2\ mínima),$$

$$r_{21}x_1 + r_{22}x_2 + r_{23}x_3 + \ldots + r_{29}x_9 \leq b_{22}\,(Restrição\ 2\ máxima),$$

$$\ldots$$

$$r_{41}x_1 + r_{42}x_2 + r_{43}x_3 + \ldots + r_{49}x_9 \geq b_{41}\,(Restrição\ 4\ mínima),$$

$$r_{41}x_1 + r_{42}x_2 + r_{43}x_3 + \ldots + r_{49}x_9 \leq b_{42}\,(Restrição\ 4\ máxima) \qquad (14)$$

Code 4 and the conversion of the mathematical formula in Python code . This code can be built in a file called *diet.py* and run in the terminal computer or in an IDE (development environment integrated).

```
# Import the import pulp tool
# Food data , a dictionary is created .
# Data = [ calories , proteins , fat ,
sodium, price ]
food = {
' burger ': [410, 24, 26, 730, 2.49],
' chicken ': [420, 32, 10, 1190, 2.89], '
ca_cante ': [560, 20, 32, 1800, 1.50], '
bat_frita ': [380, 4, 19, 270, 1.89],
'macaroni ': [320, 12, 10, 930, 2.09],
'pizza': [320, 15, 12, 820, 1.99], ' salad ':
[320, 31, 12, 1230, 2.49], ' milk ': [100, 8,
2.5, 125, 0.89], ' ice cream ': [330, 8, 10,
180, 1.59]
}
# Initializes the problem : model problem
= pulp.LpProblem ("PLMO Diet",
pulp.LpMinimize )
# Defines the Decision Variables :
quantity of each food and wasting away

# also defines the restrictions with its
min and max limits :
problem += sum([food[ food ][0] * x[ food
] for food in food]) >= 1800
problem += sum([food[ food ][0] * x[ food
] for food in food]) <= 2200
# repeats for all conditions ... problem
+= sum([food[ food ] [4] * x[ food ] for
food in food]) >= 0
problem += sum([food[ food ][4] * x[ food
] for food in food]) <= 20
# Solve the problem problem.solve ()
# Displaying you results
# Displaying results print( "Status:",
pulp.LpStatus [ prob.status ]) total_calories
, total_proteins , total_fats , price = 0, 0,
0, 0 for food in food:
qty = x[ food ]. varValue
```

```
amount of each food : 0 is minimum , 10 is
maximum quantity
x = pulp.LpProblem ("Food", food.keys (), 0,
10)
# Set the weights
weight1 = 0.5 # weight to calories
peso2 = 0.5 # weight for proteins
# Fungao goal
problem += sum( [weight1 *
food[ food ][0] * x[ food ] for food in food])
- sum( [weight2 * food[ food ][1] * x[ food

print(f"{ food }: {qty}") total_calories + =
food[ food ][0] * total_protein quantity + =
food[ food ][1] * total_fat quantity + =
food[ food ][2] * qty
price += food[ food ][4] * quantity
print("\ nTotals :")
print( f"Calories : { total_calories }") print(
f"Proteins : { total_proteins }") print( f"Fats
: { total_fats }") print( f"Fails : { price }")
```

] for food in food])	

Source: Own preparation .

Code 4. Problem Code 1 .

2.3 Evolutionary algorithms

The programation mathematics , whether is it linear or non -linear, not able to solve all you types of decision - making problems . When a problem it presents many elements complex , making difficult to build a structure systematically to find the solution great , they are needed methodologies more sophisticated . In this context , the algorithms evolutionary methods and metaheuristics search engines win emphasis . These approaches use one population of solutions candidates , who are evaluated and evolved to the over several iterations . The process is based at sampling randomization of the search space and the direction of the search according to the *fitness* value assigned to each solution candidate , generation after generation (USP, 2021; Mirjalili , 2019). algorithm evolutionary efficient and one that balances you exploration and intensification mechanisms at search for the ideal solution . He employs one strategy generic search engine , designed to explore in a effective solution space viable . Thus , a metaheuristic is used that avoids the consumption excessive resources computational , when while identifying and maintaining the best solutions within the problem search space (Mirjalili , 2019 ; Back, Fogel, Michalewicz, 2000).

One of the most acquaintances algorithms evolutionary and the algorithm genetic *algorithm* (GA), which starts with a population of solutions candidates sampled randomly in the search space (USP, 2021) (Obitko , 1998). Each solution candidate and an individual , represented computationally by a vector of attributes that the characterizes uniquely and completely . This attribute vector represents what in Biology is known per individual 's genome . Then , simulated in computer the principle of survival of the most fit , present at Darwin's theory of natural selection . Figure 3 contains a diagram of the Algorithm steps Evolutionary , in which the simulation of the survival of the most fit and a cycle that repeats itself per miscellaneous iterances , with each iteration is called one generation , including evaluation , selection and reproduction .

Source: Own elaboration .

Figure 3. Diagram describing you steps of an algorithm evolutionary .

19

The definition of the next generation , from individuals in the population current ones that already have their related fitness values (level of *fitness* of the individual), involves three basic operations (USP, 2021) (Mirjalili , 2019) (Obitko , 1998) (Coelho, 2006):

• **Selection** , which privileges The choice of individuals more able , based on decision-making processes stochastics , like you roulette methods or tournament .

• **Crossover** , which involves the formation of pairs of individuals to produce solutions Imbridas : the new individual is created per through the mixture of the characteristics of individuals progenitors . The uniform crossover and an operator very popular , with each element of the new individual 's attribute vector he has one 50% probability of coming from from parent 1 and 50% from being from of parent 2.

• **Mutation** , which inserts random disturbances us new individuals produced by crossover, allowing The local exploration of new solutions in the search space , which makes the probability of mutation generally it is made at fees lows . Normally , in literature , the mutation rate he has values low , between 1% and 20%.

Every generation , elitism can be applied , which preserves the best individual of the previous generation , if none new generation individual you have equal *fitness* or higher than the best individual from the previous generation (USP, 2021) (Mirjalili , 2019) (Obitko , 1998).

As a stopping criterion , a number can be used maximum generation or monitoring population diversity (Deb, 2011) (Coelho, 2006) (Deb; Pratap; Agarwal; Meyrivan , 2002) .

In general , the algorithms evolutionary gifts at literature they are accessible to anyone individual who contains knowledge of mathematics and computer science . Can be found in too much computing languages , mainly Python . So, in this language , libraries Pymoo , Pyevolve , Scilab , the DESDEO tool provide you algorithms evolutionary .

2.3.1 Example of algorithms evolutionary

They exist ready-made libraries and tools with semi- prepared configurations to use the algorithms evolutionary , but when you want to use them for problems specific , is concerned with adapting the code and libraries to be compatible . To understand better use of algorithms

evolutionary , an example of an algorithm simple genetics was totally implemented at Python language .

Example 1 - Algorithm genetic

You want to create one diet daily food that cares about calorie consumption . Calorie consumption restrictions for an adult range between 1800 and 2500 calories , and according to the World Health Organization , a person You must eat at least 2000 calories per day. You have access to a big food table containing the portion and calories for each food Brazilian , which can be found on the CHI website [5].

An algorithm genetic and viable for solution of this problem , as it exploits a large space for solutions and try find the solution excellent inside of this space . Suppose that the composition of this diet allows select up to 10 different food , but can repeat

---

[5]The food table with portion and calorie description can be found on this website: < https://www.chi.pt/tabela-de-calorias.htm >.

the food . Thus, the individual of the algorithm genetics and the composition of 10 foods , Table 4.

Indwduo (Food Diet - Solution Candidate)									
Food 1	Food two	Food 3	Food 4	Food 5	Food 6	Food 7	Food 8	Food 9	Food 10

Source: Own elaboration .

Table 4. Structure of the algorithm 's individuals genetic .

algorithm itself go to create these individuals and fill the 10 foods in each indwduo randomly . That is, the algorithm go create the population . Furthermore , during the process evolutionary , the algorithm do all three operations basics with individuals more ready to create the next generation .

The fitness of individuals and how fit the individual and the way to measure it represents a calculation heuristic , same as method of kin selection , reproduction and survival . So, for this problem , the fitness of the Indwduo will be how many calories the composition contains . Those who respect the calorie range [1800 , 2500] will have a high fitness value if contrary will suffer fitness penalties .

In literature , the method used for kin selection and roulette . However , for this For example , the tournament method is adopted , a method more interesting for selecting individuals . The tournament method it works as one competition of a group of participants with a number smaller than that of the population , and all individuals of the population have the same chance of being selected as participant of this tournament group . The participant more fit won the others and became the winner of the tournament , consequently , the one chosen to reproduce the population .

Finally , to generate children , the uniform crossover and mutation methods uniform . For each gene on the individual 's chromosome , it will be applied with these methods with probability fixed . The limit maximum population is ten individuals and number of generations is 5. Code 5 presents a simple example of an Algorithm Genetic of this diet problem to feed .

```python
#    Libraries
import random
import matplotlib.pyplot the plt
#    Class Individual
class Individual :
def    init   (self, chromosome =[ ]):
self .chromosome = chromosome self .total_calories = 0 self .fitness = 0
def getGene(self, index): return self.cromossomo[index]
def setGene(self, index, gene): self.cromossomo[index] = gene
def print(self):
print(f"\tCromossomo: {self.cromossomo}\n\tFitness: {self.fitness}\n\tCalorias:
{self.total_calorias}")
#    Class Algorithm Genetic classGA :
def    init   (self, food):
self .food = food self .max_povo = 10 self .max_cromo = 20 self .chance_torneio =
0.9 self .tamanho_torneio = 5 self .taxa_crossover =0.5 self .taxa_mutation = 0.3
#    Method of creating the first population
def create_population (self): people = [] for i in range( self .max_povo ):
chromosome = random. sample ( self . food , self . max_cromo ) novo_individuo =
Individual ( chromosome ) novo_individuo.fitness , novo_individuo.total_calories =
self .eval_func ( chromosome )
```

```python
people.append ( new_individual )
return people
#   Selection Method per Tournament
def tournament ( self, people ):
tournament = random. sample ( people , self . tournament_size ) best_participant = tournament [1]
are a participant in tournament :
if ( participant.fitness >= best_participant.fitness ) and ( random.random () <= self .chance_tournament ):
best_participant = participant
return best_participant
#   Method of evaluating an individual 's fitness
def eval_ func ( self, chromosome ):
total_calories = 0
fitness = 0.0
for gene in chromossomo:
total_calorias += list(gene.values())[0]
if total_calorias <= 2500 and total_calorias > 1800:
fitness += 1
if total_calorias > 2500:
fitness -= 0.25
return fitness, total_calorias
def crossover(self, ind1, ind2):
cromossomo = []
for i in range( self.max_cromo ):
if random.random () <= self .rate_crossover :
chromosome.append (ind1.getGene( i ))
else :
chromosome.append (ind2.getGene( i ))
son = Individual ( chromosome )
son.fitness , son.total_calories = self.eval_func ( chromosome )
return child
def mutation( self, individual ):
for i in range( self.max_cromo ):
if random.random () < self .rate_mutation :
individual.setGene ( i , random.choice ( self.food ))
return individual
#   Method to generate new children : selection , crossover and mutation .
def make_new_ pop ( self, people ):
children = []
while len ( children ) < ( len ( people ) or self.max_people ):
parentel = self .tournament ( people )
relative2 = relative
while parentel.chromosome == parent2.chromosome: parent2 = self.tournament ( people )
child = self .crossover (parent1, parent2) child = self .mutation ( child )
children.append ( child )
return children
def evolve ( self, people ):
#   The population create new children children = self .make _new_pop ( people ) #
Os children do part of the population people.extend ( children )
#   Order fitness ordering descending people.sort (key=lambda individual :
individual.fitness , reverse=True) # Half of the population survives , that is,
the 10 most fit survive new_people = people [ self.max_people :] print( len (
```

```python
new_people ))
return new_people
#   Example of a food database : a list of dictionaries food = [ {" hamburger ":
410}, {" ice cream ": 24}, {" potato ": 80}, {" steak_a_cavalo ": 140}, {" cod ":
122}, {" lettuce ": 19} , {"pineapple": 52}, {"banana": 85}, {" carrot ": 37}, {"
coca_cola ": 149}, {" pea ": 18}, {" spaghetti ": 192}, { " guava ": 57}, {"
lobster ": 53}, {" lingu^a ": 190}, {" ma^a ": 45}, {" mango": 91}, {" lobster ":
103} , {" yogurt ": 152}, {" lasagna ": 620}, {" integral_milk ": 152}, {" corn ":
363}, {" strawberry ": 39}, {" pastel_carne ": 165}, { " fish ": 196}, {" cucumber
": 22}, {" turkey ": 186}, {" ricotta ": 45}, {" arugula ": 7}, {" tomato ": 16},
{" crackling ": 540}, {" pork ": 398}, {" pear ": 38}, {" fried_egg ": 108}, {"
boiled_egg ": 89}, {" fanta ": 108}, {" mushroom ": 15}, {" bolo_fuba ": 192}, {"
rice ": 88}, {" beans ": 137}, {" mignon": 240}, {" picanha ": 250}, {" popcorn ":
403} , {" pao_queijo ": 75}, {"pao": 135} ]
#   Definition of some parameters
algorithm = GA( food)
EPOCHES = 5 # Generation
people = algorithm.create _population () # Creates the first population print("
Population ") print( people )
fit = [] calorie = []
#   Start the process Evolutionary
for i in range( EPOCAS): print( f"Epoca { i }") people = algorithm.evolve ( people
)
#   Results
print(" Result ")
for ind in range( len ( people )):
print( f'Individual { ind }')
people [ ind ]. print( )
fit.append ( people [ ind ].fitness)
calorie.append ( people [ ind ]. total_calories )
plt.plot (fit, calorie , ' bo ')
plt.xlabel ('Fitness')
plt.ylabel (' Calories ') plt.show ()
```

Source: Own elaboration .
Code .5 Algorithm code evolutionary .

In this algorithm , it was defined that for each generation (epoch), the population current create new children and these they are included , doubling the population . Everyone is assessed by aptitude and ten best individuals survive to the next generation . It is worth noting that there are implementations more robust for generating new individuals and selection of the best indiMduos for the next generation . This example is a method didactic to understand how is the idea of an algorithm genetic .

The result of the post -evolution of the algorithm it is present in the graph in Figure 4. It can be seen that the better individual is the one who has the highest fitness value and it approaches the amount of calories desirable for the diet (with 2767 calories and 0.75 fitness). They can there are other individuals who contain one amount of calories desirable , but if they have a lower fitness , it means that this individual it's not the best diet solution to feed in relationship to the individual who has the best fitness and close to the amount of calories respected .

23

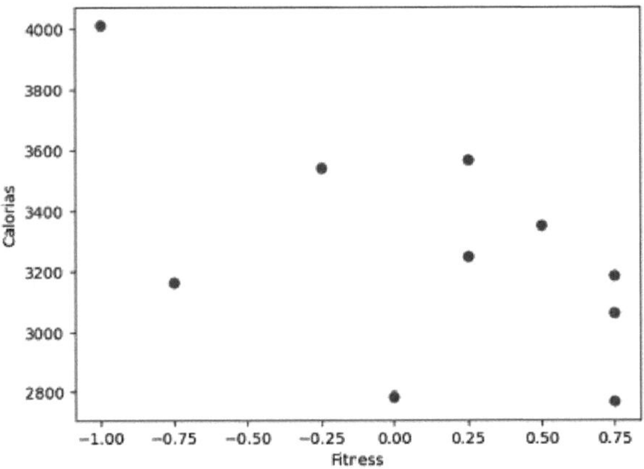

Source: Own elaboration .
Figure 4. Presentation of the result of the algorithm problem evolutionary .

2.4 Algorithms multi- objective evolutionary

When we deal with multi - objective optimization problems , adaptations they are needed us algorithms evolutionary . The objective is to guide the population of candidate solutions in towards the Pareto frontier , looking for one distributing the most uniform possible to the along this border . That provides one variety of non-dominated solutions , each one offering different compensations between objectives (Beume , Naujoks, Emmerich, 2006; Deb, Pratap, Agarwal, Meyrivan , 2002). Between the algorithms evolutionary notable for optimization multi-objective are SPEA2 (Zitzler , Laumanns , Thiele, 2001), NSGA-II (Deb, Pratap, Agarwal, Meyrivan , 2002) and SMS-EMOA (Beume , Naujoks, Emmerich, 2006).

Already exist studies that apply algorithms multi- objective evolutionary at diet problem solving to feed . An example is the use of the Differential Evolution algorithm to optimize meals daily (Zhenkui , Zhen, 2009). In this study , the algorithm considered information about the consumer , food available , restrictions nutrition and food prices . Another study used the NSGA-II algorithm to create a daily menu that maximized you nutrients essential and minimized cost (Kaldirim , Kose, 2006).

In the study with Differential Evolution, the algorithm he was programmed to determine the quantities of a pre- defined set of foods to compose meals daily . Entries included you food , while the objective functions focused at amount of energy , protein and calcium, respecting the restrictions on nutrient consumption for a person weighing 60 kg. The final result was the quantification need every food in each meal (Zhenkui , Zhen, 2009).

The second case study uses the NSGA-II as the use of a food and nutrient database , and the algorithm found the quantity of each food , forming the diet to feed desired . Furthermore , the authors also created an interface that allows insert user information and present you results . So the entries were The user 's age and gender ; and the selection of food categories . The objective functions gifts they were energy maximization and cost minimization (Kaldirim ; Kose , 2006).

In general , these algorithms gifts at literature they are also accessible to anyone individual that contains knowledge of mathematics and computer science . These too can be implemented in too much computing languages , mainly Python . The libraries Pymoo and Scilab provide several algorithms .

2.4.1 Algorithm example

These algorithms they are implemented for scenarios more complex , as they make up a set of operations to solve you problems with more than one objective . Thus, formulating a problem based at diet feed with use of these algorithms matches to a big project elaborate .

Instead of presenting an example of a diet problem food , an algorithm was described popular multi- objective evolutionary process with the aim of helping development for future projects : NSGA-II. The description of these algorithms they are at Python language .

Example 1 - NSGA-II Algorithm

The *Non-dominated Sorting Genetic Algorithm II* (NSGA-II) is a search algorithm with complexity 0 (mW 2) and contains two operations that allow the algorithm genetic to work us multi- objective scenarios : classification quickly no dominated (*fast-nondominated-sorting)* and crowding distance (crowding *distance)* . These operations stay at " selection " step of the algorithm Figure 5 contains the process evolutionary .

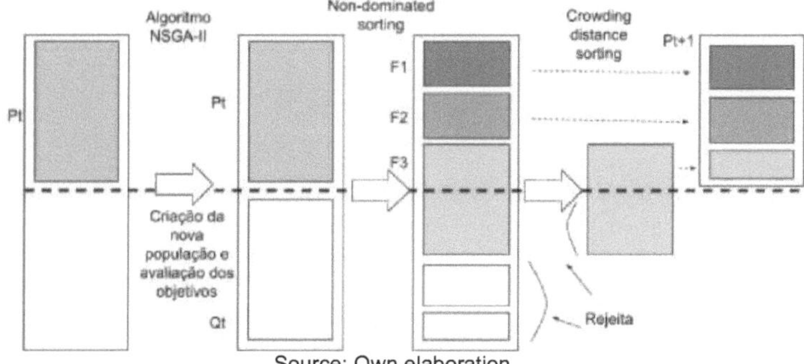

Source: Own elaboration .
Figure 5. Process evolutionary multi-objective of NSGA-II.

Given a population set (Pt), the NSGA-II algorithm starts determining the fitness of each individual . After this evaluation , a new population Qt is generated with the fitness already computed and grouped (Pt + Qt). In a stage Subsequently , the algorithm performs The *fast non-dominated* sorting operation . This process uses dominance criteria to classify you individuals in groups hierarchical , known as Fronts . Typically , the members no dominated they are positioned in the first fronts , while you dominated occupy the subsequent ones .

The algorithm then continues with the crowding distance sorting process , a metric employee at classification of individuals and selection of them for the generation subsequent . Those with values highest crowding distances are preserved , while whereas those of values lower they are discarded . Additionally , a selection technique and applied The it is metric . Completing the selection of the next generation of solutions candidates , a cycle of the process is completed evolutionary multi-objective (Pt+1).

An individual no dominated and that positioned close to the Pareto Frontier . If he it is immediately adjacent to the border and there is no other individual with superior fitness, so it is classified as one solution no dominated . In contrast , individuals dominated they are those who are far from the Pareto Frontier , there are other individuals who have more fitness suitable in comparison . In others words , these are dominated and, consequently , not represent the solutions great in the search space .

How to identify you indiMduos , or solution , if they are dominated or no dominated and a comparison between objectives of two solutions . Imagine we have an optimization problem with multiple objectives and we are comparing two solutions , A and B. A is said dominate B, if A is at any less so good how much B in all you objectives and better in for the least one of them. If A dominates B, then B and one solution dominated in relation to A. However , if A does not dominates B and B does not dominates A, then both solutions they are no calls dominated by each other . None of the solutions are strictly better than the other in all you goals . Code 6 is the pseudocode of the two operations of the NSGA-II algorithm and Code 7 presents the algorithm full of a problem binary in maximize you numbers 1s and 0s.

fast-nondominated-sorting

for each p $\in$ Population :	creates a set of solutions dominated create one solution count dominated If p dominates q: q enters the set of dominated if q dominates add the count of dominants of p if not have none score p belongs to the first Front starts the Front count creates another set for other Fronts

$$S_p = \varnothing$$

$$n_p = 0$$

para cada $q \in$ *População*:

   se $(p \prec q)$ então:

$$S_p = S_p \cup q$$

   senão se $(q \prec p)$ então

$$n_p = n_p + 1$$

se $n_p = 0$ então:

$$p_{rank} = 1$$

$$F1 = F1 \cup \{p\}$$

i = 1

enquanto $Fi \neq \varnothing$:

   $Q = \varnothing$

   para cada $p \in Fi$:

     para cada $q \in Si$:

$$n_q = n_q - 1$$

     se $n_q = 0$ então:

$$q_{rank} = i + 1$$

	crowding distance
$Q = Q \cup \{q\}$ $i = i + 1$ $Fi = Q$ $I = \|I\|$ para cada i: $I[i]_{dist} = 0$ para cada objetivo m: $I = sort(I, m)$ $I[1]_{dist} = I[l]_{dist} = \infty$ de $i = 2$ à $(l - 1)$:	number of solutions I defines the distance from I[i] = 0 performs one organization for each goal defines the Limits as infinite performs a from-to loop

$$I[i]_{dist} = I[i]_{dist} + (I[i + 1].m - I[i - 1].m)/(f_m^{max} - f_m^{min})$$

Source: Deb, 2002.

Code 6. NSGA-II pseudocode .

```
import random
class Individual :
def    init   (self, size ):
self.genoma = [random.choice([0, 1]) for _ in range(tamanho)] self.objetivos =
self.evaluate() # valores objetivos self.rank =0     # rank da fronteira
self.crowding_distance = 0 # crowding distance
def evaluate(self):
#   Defines a function that evaluates the individual 's fitness # depends on the
problem specific .
#   Example : maximize the number of 1s and 0s: [qty of 1s, qty of 0s] return
[sum( self.genome ), len ( self.genome ) - sum( self.genome )]
def dominates ( self, other):
#   A domina B quando:
andC = True
orC = False
for first, second in zip(self.objetivos, outro.objetivos): # Cond_E = Ax <= Bx E
Ay <= By andC = andC and first <= second # Cond_OU = Ax <= Bx OU Ay < By orC = orC
or first < second
#   Cond_E E Cond_OU
return ( andC and orC )
def initialize_population ( population_size , genome_size ) :
return [ Individual ( genome_size ) for _ in range( population_size )]
def crossover( parent1, parent2):
crossover_point = random.randint (1, len ( parentel.genome ) - 1)
son = Individual ( len ( parent1.genome))
```

```python
son2 = Individual ( len ( parent1.genome))
son1.genome = parent1.genome [: crossover _point ] +
parent2.genome[ crossover_point :]
son2.genome = parent2.genome [: crossover _point ] +
parent1.genome[ crossover_point :]
return son , son2
def change( individual , change_rate ):
for i in range( len ( individual.genome )):
if random.random () < change_rate :
individual.genome [ i ] = 1 - individual.genome [ i ]
def tournament ( population , k=2 ):
#   Select k individuals randomly from the population
selection = random. sample ( population , k)
#   Return the best of these k individuals based on rank and crowding_distance
selecao.sort (key=lambda individual :
( individuo.rank , -individuo.crowding_distance ))
return selecao[0]
def crowding_operator(individuo1, individuo2):
if (individuo1.rank < individuo2.rank) or ( (individuo1.rank == individuo2.rank)
and (individuo1.crowding_distance > individuo2.crowding_distance)):
return True
else:
return False
def fast_non_dominated_sort(populacao):
fronts = [[]]
S = [[] for _ in range( len ( population ))] # list of individuals dominated per
each individual
n = [0 for _ in range( len ( population ))] # number of individuals that dominate
each individual
#   Step 1: Prepare each pair of solutions na populace
for p_index , p in enumerate( population ):
for q_index , q in enumerate( population ):
if p.domina (q):
S[ p_index ].append (q)
Elif lady (p):
n[ p_index ] += 1
#   If 'p' is not dominated per any other, he belongs to the first border
if n[ p_index ] == 0:
p.rank = 0
if p not in fronts[ 0]: fronts[0].append(p)
#   Step 2: Create the next ones fronts
i = 0
while len(fronts[i]) > 0: next_front = []
for p_indice, p in enumerate(fronts[i]):
for q_indice, q in S[p_indice]: n[q_indice] -= 1 if n[q_indice] <= 0:
q.rank = i + 1
next_front.append(q) i += 1
fronts.append(next_front)
print( f"Size of fronts = { len (fronts)}")
#   Remove the last frontier empty and return the fronts fronts.pop ( )
print( len (fronts)) return fronts
def calculate_crowding_distance ( front , population ):
#   Distance initialization for everyone you individuals at border for individual
in front:
```

```python
individual.crowding _distance = 0
#    For each goal
n_objectives = len (front[0 ]. objectives ) for obj_index in range( n_objectives
):
#    Order the individuals based on objective current
front = sorted( front, key=lambda x: x.objectives [ obj_index ])
#    Defines the distance limits as infinite front[ 0]. crowding_distance =
float('inf') front[-1]. crowding_distance = float('inf')
#    For all the other individuals , calculate the distance like the difference
#    between the values of neighbors ' goals
obj_range = front[-1 ]. objectives [ obj_index ] - front[0]. objectives [
obj_index ] for i in range(1, len (front) - 1):
if obj_range == 0: # preventing division by zero distance = 0
else:
distance = (front[i+1 ]. objectives [ obj_index ] - front[i-1]. objectives [
obj_index ]) / obj_range
front[ i ]. crowding _distance += distance
def nsga2( population_size =5, epochs =2, genome_size =10, mutation_rate =0.01):
population = initialize_population ( population_size , genome_size )
for epoca in range( epocas ): print( f"Epoca { epoca }") # Ordering no dominated
and calculation of crowding distance fronts = fast_non_dominated_sort ( population
) for front in fronts:
calculate_crowding_distance ( front , population )
#    Generation of the next population nova_populacao = [] while len (
nova_population ) < size_population : parent1 = tournament ( population ) parent2
= tournament ( population ) son1, son2 = crossover( parent1, parent2)
mutate(filho1, mutation_rate ) mutate(filho2, mutation_rate ) son1.objetivos =
son1.evaluate() son2.objectives = son2.evaluate() nova_populacao.extend ([son1,
son2])
population = new_population [: size _population ]
return fronts[ 0]
# Execution
result = nsga2()
for individual in result : print( individuo.genome )
```

Source: Own elaboration .
Code 7. NSGA-II Code in Python language .

2.5 Optimization bilevel

When formulating a problem mathematician , the choice of resolution method depends on the nature and objectives of the problem . If he is identified as a single - objective optimization problem , the approach appropriate would be single- objective linear programming or programming non -linear mono- objective , case involved elements no linear . On the other hand , problems with multiple goals inseparable require optimization methods multiobjective . Already problems combinatorics , which require one approach heuristic to find solutions , can be better solved with algorithms evolutionary . Furthermore , problems that present characteristics mixed , like be simultaneously combinatorial and multi- objective , can be addressed by the Optimization strategy Binivel.Em organizations public and private , optimization and decision - making processes usually to occur in big scale and in a hierarchical manner . That means that the solutions or decisions sockets per one top mobile authority (the Hder) to optimize your goals they are influenced by responses from the lower level (the follower), who seeks optimize your own results . This dynamic

30

hierarchical can be modeled mathematically , where the method employee on the upper level issues guidelines for the lower level aiming reach your objectives , and the lower level , for your time , provides solutions found by another method to the upper furniture .

The formulation overview of an optimization problem bimvel multiobjective takes the form (Sinha et al., 2018).

$$\min_x F_2(x, y)]$$

sujeito a

$$G(x, y) \leq 0$$

$$\min_y f(x, y)$$

sujeito a

$$g(x, y) \leq 0 \tag{15}$$

The top - level decision maker also called Hder, has control about the variables x and take your decision first . The lower - level decision maker also called follower , controls the variables y and reacts to the Leader's decision , with the variables y they are defined in response to each x proposed .

In the context of the diet problem food , for For example , the variables x define which foods irao composing the diet (being a problem combinatorial) and the variables y specify the quantity best of each food selected in x (being a programming problem mathematics). This context will be more in depth in the next chapter , where works on the diet problem feed in the optimization scenario bi-mobile and multi- purpose .

## Chapter 3

Diet problem to feed bi-mobile and multi- purpose

This chapter presents a master 's project developed for the author , focused at exploration of optimization bi-mobile and multi- objective in the context of the diet problem to feed . The project is characterized by the creation of a recommendation system for diets personalized , which provides one range of menus diaries , each containing four meals . These menus they are optimized to meet restrictions nutritional defined per experts , taking in consideration of composition nutritional and caloric content of foods and the pre- established categorization of groups food .

The methodology employee in this study involves the formulation of programming problems mathematics , using the Non - dominated Sorting Genetic Algorithm II (NSGA -II) and Linear Programming using the GUROBI tool. These approaches allow one optimization simultaneous and multifaceted objectives dietetics , leading to the development of menus that represent solutions efficient within the Pareto frontier for the diet to feed . Each menu proposed aims to achieve a balance between the various needs nutritional and preferences individual .

Over the years , the field of Diet have seen a proliferation of methods mathematicians proposed to resolve your classic problem . This section of the book offers an overview of these approaches , highlighting as each one contributes to improving solution strategies . Given the diversity of proposals , a comparability challenge arises : many times It's not clear how many different methods intersect , complement or contradict each other . The search in diet food and broad and complex , marked per one variety of goals and approaches methodologies . Each study addresses the topic with nuances and perspectives own , making the field dynamic , but complex to establish compareQdes direct .

One of the aspects yet underexploited and the problem of diet to feed multi-objective , which seeks balance simultaneously criteria as nutrition , cost and preferences individual . Furthermore , the approaches bilevels , in which decisions at a higher level (such as guidelines nutritional) affect and are affected per choices at a lower level (like habits food individual), also deserve emphasis . This multiplicity of methods and objectives highlights the wealth and potential yet unexplored field, encouraging researchers The to explore more deeply into the complexities of the diet to feed .

In this section , a scenario is discussed diet complex food , involving both the problem combinatorial multi-objective regarding programming mono objective linear mathematics . The challenge here and propose one variety of diets food for the user , allowing him to choice one of these diets and follow it with guidance from a nutritionist . The objective is to develop a diet recommendation system food that incorporates expert advice in nutrition and feeding .

3.1 Scope of the problem

Address the Diet Problem feed with a perspective bi-mobile and multi- purpose and highly relevant . This is due to the complexity inherent to balance miscellaneous restrictions and objectives that comprise one diet , which generates one vast combination of possible food composites . Furthermore , it is crucial to consider The interrelationship between specifications nutritional and caloric presets for the diet and properties individual for each food . It is worth highlighting that the acceptance of the diet for the individual and essential . That suggests that a menu diversified , with multiple dish options , tends to be more attractive and easy to follow than a diet restricted to a few op^des . Thus, a recommendation system for diets food and appropriate for this scope that, in addition to meeting The these properties mentioned , provides a menu varied . However , such system requires information detailed about you food as well as guidelines dietetics provided by an expert in the area.

To address adequately the peculiarities of the diet problem feed and prevent complications arising from specific situations , established the scope of the problem with the following conditions :

1. For food and nutrient information in order to construct decision variables and restrictions , these are used the Brazilian Food Composition Table Version 4 - TACO4 (NEPA, 2006), the Diana Recommendation and Restrictions tables Adequate (National Institutes of Health, 2011) and the Canada Dietary Reference Intakes tables (2010).

2. The focus was considered in one person adult (from 18 to 35 years old).

3. A Diet specification is for 24 hours. Four meals daily they were defined for this presentation , involving breakfast , lunch , snack and dinner , and it was specified , for each one of these meals , the presence of categories specific foods , forming a vector of size fixed able to indicate you foods gifts in one diet daily , to be selected within your categories specific .

Adopting the optimization strategy binivel , there are two levels . The top level has a multi- objective problem combinatorial with two goals conflicting to be simultaneously optimized . One involving meeting an energy distribution standard purchased and quantity of food to the throughout the meals and another involving the total cost of purchasing and preparing the four meals daily . The lower level of this optimization strategy bilevel has a linear single objective problem . The goal is to maximize The total possible energy food combination sent for the higher level .

The development of a multi - objective recommendation system for diets food involves The information integration nutritional detailed about you food and application structured structure of restrictions dietetics provided per experts . On level operational , for each composition proposal food , a programming *solver* is used mathematics to determine the ideal quantity of each food item , approaching the problem from a mono objective perspective . A key tool for this optimization and Gurobi , a private solver that meets you requirements of that project (https://www.gurobi.com/) (GUROBI, 2021). Is important highlight that there are other *solvers* with functionalities equivalents that also could be used .

On level strategically , the *Non-dominated Sorting Genetic Algorithm II* (NSGA-II) is employed to explore the space of composition alternatives food , addressing the problem as a challenge multi- objective combinatorics . The search space for this problem combinatorial and defined when establishing previously the food categories available , the foods candidates in each category and the composition of the four meals daily rates : breakfast , lunch , snack and dinner . As an example , imagine 12 food categories , each one with 20 options different (for simplicity , the same number of foods per category). If breakfast includes 4 categories foods distinct , lunch 6, snack 3 and dinner 5, so we have a total of 18 foods many different consumed in one day. That results in one search space cardinality of approximately 2.62×10^{23} . Many studies at literature already define the food list in advance or carry out the search in a limited set of options . In this presentation , however , it investigates a space very more broad , seeking identify food lists diversified products that produce solutions efficient for the diet problem .

This method creates an optimization problem bimable , where , for each food list proposal by NSGA-II, Gurobi determines the ideal amount of each food . In this way, the system generates diet recommendations daily complete and balanced , incorporating you aspects nutritional and preferences individual .

3.2 Understanding the System

It is clear that it was necessary to develop a system with several properties and functionalities . To understand how it works of this system , a flow of information was created , allowing the understanding of communication between two algorithms , in question that NSGA- II calls Gurobi all once a solution candidate (composition proposal food , or that is , a subset of foods selected) needs to be evaluated . Your flow it must be a cycle , starting and ending with the user . Figure 6 shows The illustration of this information flow in top- mobile perspective : the user insert the data of interest , capable of specifying the diet feed , and receive at the end a list of solutions efficient (with varied *trade-* offs between multiple objectives) , each specifying which foods consume in each one of four refeigtees daily , and in what quantity . This list of solutions candidates alternatives and capable of meeting all restrictions imposed by the diet , unless there is solutions It is possible that the pair [NSGA-II + Gurobi] can meet .

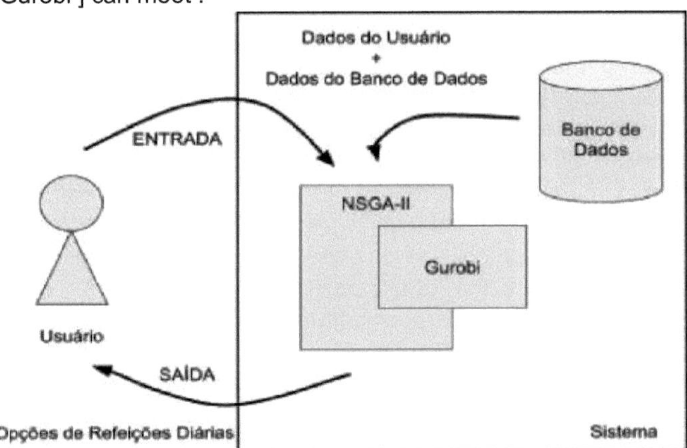

Source: Own preparation .
Figure 6. Information flow adopted for the diet recommendation system , formulated as an optimization problem bilevel .

Through of that concept presented , the software project was modeled , which was designed based on three modules (see Figure 7):

1. Interface, responsible for collecting data at system input and presenting solutions at output to the user ;

2. Programming mathematics and optimization multiobjective , that will integrate programming tools mathematics Gurobi and the optimization algorithm evolutionary multi-

objective NSGA-II;

3.   Database, responsible per store the tables nutritional requirements of foods and dietary contour conditions , in addition to defining controls for communication between the database and too much system modules .

Prодгатаdйо interface of Database Optimization

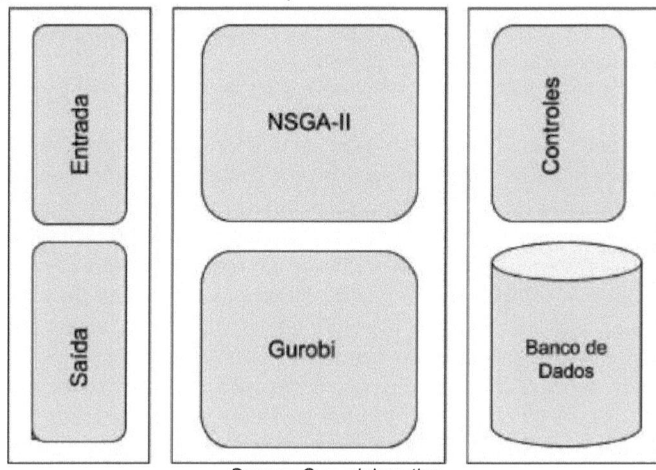

Source: Own elaboration

Figure 7. Modules constituents of the optimization system multipurpose for diets food , formulated as an optimization problem binlvel .

At the core of this diet recommendation system food , there is the Interface module, a component that captures preferences user 's food for the four meals daily rates : breakfast , lunch , snack and dinner . These preferences , along with other relevant user data , are inserted into the system , which forwards them to the Database module through Controls . This process is essential to ensure consistency and ordering data, creating a package information that is the basis for operations subsequent ones .

The next stage involves the Optimization Programming module , where you NSGA-II and Gurobi algorithms they are posts in agao . Starting with NSGA-II, the system process you data packet parameters to generate one population initial of possible diets , each one representing one combination complete set of food for meals daily . Using fast-nondominated-sorting and crowding-distance techniques , NSGA-II embarks in a process evolutionary multiobjective , seeking solutions optimal and diverse (Deb et al., 2002; Oliveira et al., 2018).

However , for the evolution is carried out effectively , and it is essential determine the quantities best of each food in the diets proposals . This task is assigned to the Gurobi solver , which operates on mobile lower bilevel of optimization . For each solution candidate generated by NSGA-II, Gurobi solves a linear programming problem , defining the ideal quantity of each food , so as not to transgress restrictions nutritional imposed , including you tolerance intervals for each nutrient specified . In this process bimvel , the Gurobi adopt its own objective function , focused at maximizing the total energy of the diet , aligned with the fundamental objective of any

35

dietary regime : acquisition adequate energy .

At the top level , NSGA-II operates with two objective functions distinct and conflicting , reflecting the complexity and challenges inherent to the formulation of diets optimized . Although others objective functions could be incorporated to NSGA-II, the choose two of them, in this instance , no compromises the generality and effectiveness of the proposal . The two objective functions conflicting they are :

1. Total cost to acquire and prepare the four meals daily ;
2. Degree of compliance with a standard of energy distribution and quantity of food to the throughout meals .

This process repeats itself , generation after generation , until a stopping criterion it is reached . Here we define as stopping criterion a number maximum generations . Finally , the system deliver the solutions non-dominated in the Output in the Interface module , and the results they are formatted in one meal list daily for the user .

The NSGA-II algorithm requires the definition of hyperparameters to perform the search multiobjective . Population size and operator fees genetics they were defined in values already substantiated at literature about algorithms evolutionary . They were considered 100 individuals for population size and selection per five-a- side tournament indMduos . As for the operators genetics , the crossover operator *was* used uniform , with a 50% chance, and the mutation operator uniform , with a 30% chance (Mirjalili , 2019) (USP, 2021). Food data for the database

To the operation effective of this system , it is essential to obtain information detailed about you foods . These data were extracted from the Brazilian Food Composition Table Version 4 (TACO4), a national referendum consolidated . TACO4 categorizes you foods in many different groups , providing no just the classification , but also you nutrients associated with each food . This base includes a total of 597 foods distributed in 15 categories . Furthermore , each food entry contains 24 nutrients distinct and 4 characteristics additional attributes , totaling 28 attributes . Table 5 presents a summary of the data contained at TACO4.

Categories TACO4 food					
Cereals and derivatives	Vegetables , Vegetables and Derivatives	Fruits and Derivatives	Fats and Oils	Fish and Fruits Sea	Subtotal
63	99	96	14	50	322
Meat and derivatives	Milk and dairy products	Drinks Alcoholic and Non- Alcoholic	Eggs and Egg Products	Products Apucarados	Subtotal
123	24	14	7	20	188
Miscellaneous	Other Processed Foods	Foods Prepared	Legumes and derivatives	Nuts and Seeds	Subtotal
9	5	32	30	11	87
Total					597
Units of the 24 Food Nutrients (100g)					
Attribute	Unit	Attribute	Unit	Attribute	Unit
Protema	g	Energy	kcal/KJ	Cholesterol	mg
Lipids	g	Carbohydrate	g	Dietary Fiber	g
calcium	mg	Ashes	g	Manganes	mg
Magnesium	mg	Iron	mg	Phosphorus	mg
Potassium	mg	Sodium	mg	Cobre	mg
Zinc	mg	Retinol	mcg	C vitamin	mg
KING	mcg	RAE	mcg	Thiamine	mg
Riboflavin	mg	Pyridoxine	mg	Niacin	mg

Source: NEPA, 2006

Table 5. TACO4 scope of information .

In addition , nutrient restriction tables food , as cited by (NCBI, 2011) and (Canada, 2010), establish values minimum , recommended and maximum nutrient consumption , segmenting them according to tracks ages and genders . This wide range of references enables the development of systems that address the needs nutritional to the throughout the various phases biological approaches of the individual , thus differentiating themselves from more restrictive often found at literature .

These references list recommendations for a total of 29 nutrients , including vitamins , salts minerals and macronutrients , structured in five life stage categories . However , there was a need to complete some gaps in these tables with information from the Canada Dietary Reference Intakes (2010), especially when it came to determining values maximum consumption insurance .

Table 6 summarizes the specifications of the restriction tables nutritional mentioned . It is crucial to emphasize that modulation of these tolerance intervals nutritional must be conducted per experts in the area, considering the peculiarities of each diet . The objective is to provide a tool that allows the personalization and flexibility of these diets , adapting to one vast range of needs and scenarios .

These sources of information they are great importance and can be of great research utilities future in the field of diet to feed or studies nutritional .

Life Stage Groups					
Babies	**Children**	**Men**	**Women**	**Pregnancy**	**Lactation**
0 - 6 months	13 years	9-13 years	14-18 years old	14-18 years old	14-18 years old
6-12 months	6-12 years	19-30 years old	31 - 50 years	19-30 years old	19-30 years old
		51 - 70 years	71 or more	31 - 50 years	31 - 50 years
Units of the 29 Food Nutrients					
Attribute	**Unit**	**Attribute**	**Unit**	**Attribute**	**Unit**
calcium	mg/d	Chrome	mg/d	Copper	md/d
Fluoride	mg/d	Iodine	pg /d	Iron	mg/d
Magnesium	mg/d	Manganese	mg/d	Molybdenum	pg /d
Phosphorus	mg/d	Selenium	pg /d	Zinc	mg/d
Potassium	g/d	Sodium	mg	Chloreto	g/d
Vitamin A	j g /d	Vitamin C	mg/d	Vitamin D	pg /d
Vitamin E	mg/d	Vitamin K	pg /d	Tiamina	mg/d
Riboflavin	mg/d	Niacin	mg/d	Vitamin B6	pg /d
Folate	pg /d	Vitamin B12	pg /d	Acidity pantothenic	mg/d
Biotin	pg /d	The hill	mg/d	**Total**	**29**

Source: NCBI, 2010

Table 6. Scope of information in the Nutrient Restriction Table .

3.3 Solution candidate

They exist food categories good consolidated at literature and that each snack he must take one food of each one of the categories that compose it , and considered here that a snack no admit more than one food from one same category . Also it was left defined in scope of this work that a diet refers over a 24-hour period , when will occur four Meals : breakfast , lunch , snack and dinner . How are specified a priori the categories of foods that make up each meal , whose quantity and given by $n_{café}$, n_{alm} , n_{lan} and n_{Jan} , then it is concluded that a solution candidate will be a vector of size fixed , as the number of foods in the diet is given by $n_{total} = n_{café} + n_{alm} + n_{lan} + n_{jan}$.

He is like this good characterized by nature combinatorics of the diet problem , since each of the $total\ n$ foods must be chosen among those ones available in the respective food categories recipients in each snack . In the absence of prior preferences or filters that impose the presence or absence of any food specifically , the choice within each food category he must follow one probability uniform .

Even if you know the entire composition nutrition of food candidates and if you have objectives and restrictions good defined for the diet , without defining the quantities individual for each food chosen , nothing can be claim about the quality of a certain solution candidate .

Therefore , in addition to the problem combinatorial , enough challenging , there is an associated linear programming problem : given the composition proposal food in the diet , what and how much best to consider for each food , respecting the restrictions and boundary conditions imposed ?

While most of the recommendation systems for diets nourishments of literature , which also operate under a perspective multi-objective , assign it is task to the algorithm itself evolutionary , in this case here would be NSGA-II, the programming problem mathematics associated with each solution candidate proposal by NSGA-II and resolved for the Gurobi , after conceiving the diet problem as being optimization bilevel .

It is evident that the number of meals daily allowance and the number of food categories per meal go depend on the application , and the values adopted here and in experimental part of this work must serve just as an example , you can vary arbitrarily , according to the user 's interests .

In the following example , there were twelve food categories were considered (C1 to C12) and $n_{café} = n_{alm} = n_{lan} = n_{jan} = 3$. Also they were considered 7 nutrients that will compose the diet contour guidelines , having their information for each food from the twelve food categories . A solution structure candidate , to be proposed by NSGA-II, and presented at Table 7. Assuming they were selected as foods that make up breakfast Cake Mix (chosen among the options in Category C1), Beverage Lactea (chosen among the options in Category C2) and Jabuticaba (chosen among the options in Category C3), Table 8 contains part of the information that will be used for the Gurobi to define the quantity of each food that makes up the diet , all listed in a vector fixed size $total\ n = 12$.

Cafe da Manha			AlmoQO			Jantar			Lunch		
C1	C2	C3	C4	C5	C6	C7	C8	C9	C10	C11	C12

Fonte: Elabora^ao propria.

Table 7. Size vector structure fixed that represents one solution candidate .

Breakfast					
C1	Cereal	C2	Milk	C3	Fruit

Name	Cake Mix	Name	Drink Lactea	Name	Jabuticaba
Energy	418 kcal	Power	55.16 kcal	Power	58.05 kcal
Pre?o	R$6.16	Pre?o	R$2.13	Pre?o	R$ 0.51
Protema	6.2g	Protema	1.5g	Protema	0.6 g
Soccer	59 mg	Soccer	89 mg	Soccer	8mg
Fiber Food	1.7 mg	Fiber Food	0.29 mg	Fiber Food	2.3mg
Iron	1.12g	Iron	0.01 g	Iron	0.09g
Vitamin A	0.0 mcg	Vitamin A	0.01 mcg	Vitamin A	0.0 mcg

Source: Own elaboration . NEPA data, 2011.

Table 8. Composition of the Breakfast structure .

Once specified you foods within each category at solution candidate , for the four meals (here it is illustrated just breakfast) , Gurobi will use the food composition at definition of quantity optimum to be assigned to each food .

3.4 Preparation of NSGA-II

Serao considered here two goals conflicts in NSGA-II, which must be met simultaneously . Are they :

1.   Cost sum of acquisition and preparation of all meals , to be minimized , defined as *Cost* ;

2.   Degree of follow -up of referral guidelines for food distribution to the over four meals , to be maximized , defined as *Concentration* . This objective send to the meal performance , but is converted to minimization by taking the negative of its value . Yours conception he was partially inspired by the study preliminary accomplished by Ferreira (2017), in your initiation work scientific .

The motivation for taking the full *cost of* meals as one of the objectives of NSGA-II and its ado^ao majority at literature , since minimizing the cost of the diet is generally taken as one of the objectives to be optimized (Santos; Sichieri ; Darmon et al., 2018) (Vieux; Maillot; Drewnowski, 2019) (Dooren, 2018) (Patil; Kasturi, 2016) (Sklan ; Dariel, 1992) (Oliveira; Caldeira;

The second objective , called Concentration , basically verifies that the distribution of food and energy it is balanced daytime . A idea and avoid that, for For example , all food is consumed only at lunch , leaving other side meals . Imagine power to fulfill all the needs of a diet just with what you eat for lunch , without need breakfast , snack or to have lunch . That it would n't be much practical , right ? Therefore , we seek with this goal ensure a balance , focusing more at lunch and dinner as the main meals , but that can be adjusted according to what the experts recommend.Interesting note that this objective of *concentrating* on can sometimes come in in conflict with *Cost* . For example , prepare just one meal , such as lunch , and more fast and can be more cheaper than preparing four meals . Furthermore , some foods they are more cheaper than others, and if we were just in them , we could save , but it would not be balanced . So , the *Concentration* helps to ensure that let's be focusing just us foods more cheap .

Evidently , other objectives and more than two goals conflicting could be considered , keeping the rest intact stages of the methodology , although with some impact on the search cost , in the case of more than two goals .

For each solution candidate , both objective functions must be evaluated , in order to position it in the space of objectives . So that it is possible to assess any of the objective functions , it is necessary to define no just you foods that make up the diet (information provided by NSGA-II), but the quantity of each food (information provided for the Gurobi).

mathematical equations of the NSGA-II objectives can be observed in the Equations 16 to 21. The formula for the first objective function is a sum of the quantities of each food multiplied for the your cost (of acquisition and preparation), presented at Equation 16. The formula for the second objective function is a sum of four terms : *energy distribution (dE)* , weight distribution (dP) , *quantity distribution (dQ)* and weight score (nP) (Equation 17).

$$Custo = n_{caf}\, custo_{caf} + n_{alm}\, custo_{alm} + n_{jan}\, custo_{jan} + n_{lan}\, custo_{lan} \quad (16)$$

where $n_{caf|alm|jan|lan}$ is the quantity of food in the meals breakfast , lunch , dinner and snack , respectively and $custo_{caf|alm|jan|lan}$ is cost corresponding food in the breakfast , lunch , dinner and snack meals , respectively .

$$Concentração = -1\,(dE + dP + dQ + nP) \quad (17)$$

The *energy distribution (dE)* (Equation 18) and the *weight distribution (dP)* (Equation 19) are associated with referendum conditions for energy distribution purchased and quantity of food consumed to the throughout meals , as informed at Table 9. These referendum leads were initially proposals in Ferreira (2017). As already mentioned , the motivation is in the fact that they seek diets that don't concentrate energy purchased and quantity of food in one or two meals among the four of the day. If the meal answer the referendum , it receives a value of 1 point , receiving 0 if contrary . After evaluating every meal , add the meal points and divide by the total amount of meals in order to have one final grade in the range between 0 and 1. Evidently , these Referendum conditions in Table 9 can be adjusted for the specialist , according to the demands of the application .

Meals	Power Distribution (relative to Total Energy)	Weight Distribution
Refeições	Distribuição de Energia (relativo à Energia Total)	Distribuição de Peso
Café da Manhã (Caf)	$15\% < energia_{caf} < 35\%$	$300g < quantidade_{caf} < 500g$
Almoço (Alm)	$15\% < energia_{alm} < 40\%$	$400g < quantidade_{alm} < 600g$
Jantar (Jan)	$15\% < energia_{jan} < 40\%$	$400 < quantidade_{jan} < 600g$
Lanche (Lan)	$5\% < energia_{lan} < 15\%$	$300g < quantidade_{lan} < 500g$

Source: Own elaboration .

Table 9. Referendum conditions for energy distribution purchased and quantity of food consumed to the over four meals daily .

$$dE = \frac{eCaf + eAlm + eJan + eLan}{total\ de\ refeicao}$$

$$s.t.$$

$$eCaf = \begin{cases} 1, & se\ 15\% <= \frac{energia_{caf}}{energia\ total}100\% <= 35\% \\ 0, & caso\ contrario \end{cases}$$

$$eAlm = \begin{cases} 1, & se\ 15\% <= \frac{energia_{alm})}{energia\ total}100\% <= 40\% \\ 0, & caso\ contrario \end{cases}$$

$$eJan = \begin{cases} 1, & se\ 15\% <= \frac{energia_{jan}}{energia\ total}100\% <= 40\% \\ 0, & caso\ contrario \end{cases}$$

$$eLan = \begin{cases} 1, & se\ 5\% <= \frac{energia_{lan}}{energia\ total}100\% <= 15\% \\ 0, & caso\ contrario \end{cases}$$

$$(18)$$

$$dP = \frac{pCaf + pAlm + pJan + pLan}{total\ de\ refeicao}$$

$$s.t.$$

$$pCaf = \begin{cases} 1, & se\ 300g <= quantidade_{caf} <= 500g \\ 0, & caso\ contrario \end{cases}$$

$$pAlf = \begin{cases} 1, & se\ 400g <= quantidade_{lan} <= 600g \\ 0, & caso\ contrario \end{cases}$$

$$pJan = \begin{cases} 1, & se\ 400g <= quantidade_{jan} <= 600g \\ 0, & caso\ contrario \end{cases}$$

$$pLan = \begin{cases} 1, & se\ 300g <= quantidade_{lan} <= 500g \\ 0, & caso\ contrario \end{cases}$$

$$(19)$$

The third calculation , *distribution of quantity* (dQ) , and the average quantity of food actually considered for the Gurobi , for each solution candidate (Equation 20). In other words , one point is added for each food that appears in quantity bigger or equal to 1 unit (usually equivalent to a portion of 100 grams), dividing by the total number of foods that make up the candidate solution in order to have one final grade in the range between 0 and 1. The less food o Gurobi take advantage of , among those who make up the solution candidate , the lower *the food distribution score* will be .

$$dQ = \frac{1}{n}\sum_{i=0}^{n} qtdUnitaria(quantidade_{x_i})$$

$$s.t.$$

$$qtdUnitaria(quantidade_{x_i}) = \begin{cases} 1, & se\ quantidade_{x_i} >= 1 \\ 0, & caso\ contrario \end{cases}$$

$$(20)$$

Finally , the fourth calculation , *weight note* (nP), and a function also heuristic formed per one piecewise linear function , which was inspired in the way fuzzy rules are activated (Equation 21) (Cavallaro, 2015). The score varies between -1 and +1, with +1 when the total weight of food from all meals is between 900 g and 2100 g, considered one normal range . For values below and above of this interval , the note suffers one linear fall , being more accentuated for values below 900 g. It is noticed that this calculation he can result in a negative value ; or be the assessment of the weight of the composition he can penalize the final value of the objective function .

Notice that this heuristic also can be edited for the user , being possible reset all your behavior .

$$nP = nota, \text{ onde} -1 <= nota <= 1$$
$$s.t.$$
$$pesoTotal = peso_{caf} + peso_{alm} + peso_{jan} + peso_{lan}$$

$$nota = \begin{cases} -1, & \text{se } pesoTotal <= 0g \\ -\left(\frac{450 - pesoTotal}{450}\right), & \text{se } 0g < pesoTotal < 450g \\ \frac{pesoTotal - 450}{450}, & \text{se } 450g < pesoTotal < 900g \\ 1, & \text{se } 900g <= pesoTotal <= 2100g \\ \frac{3150 - pesoTotal}{1050}, & \text{se } 1500g < pesoTotal <= 3150g \\ -\left(\frac{pesoTotal - 3150}{1050}\right), & \text{se } 3150g < pesoTotal < 4200g \\ -1, & \text{se } pesoTotal >= 4200g \end{cases} \qquad (21)$$

mathematical formula of the second objective function with the four terms and presented at Equation 17, with the formulas for each individual term are presented at sequence . It is noticed that this objective , after all the sums of the scores , is converted to a negative value , as we want to minimize This one goal at search for NSGA-II solutions . Figure 8 illustrates the behavior of the term *weight* , as already described verbatim .

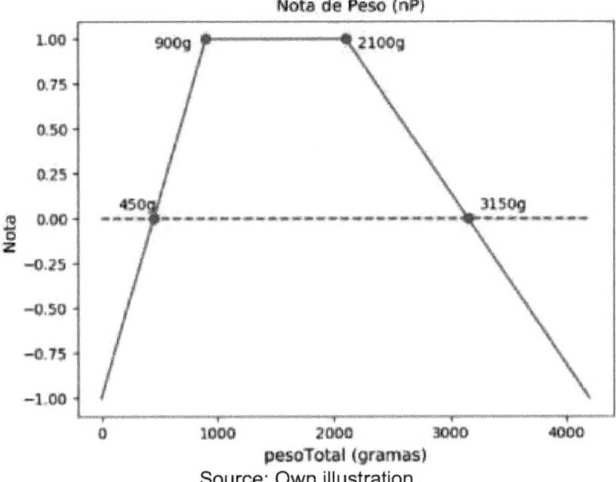

Source: Own illustration .

Figure 8. Term behavior *weight note (nP)* , which is a piecewise linear function , penalizing the grade for cases in which the total weight of the food consumed to the over four meals he is below 900 g and above 2100 g.

3.6 Develop and program linear mathematics gurobi

Using an algorithm evolutionary , we seek find the best solutions for the user 's diet considering two objectives : total cost and balance at food distribution . The algorithm eat creating one population initial solution . These solutions they are generated randomly and, in then , they are enhanced using techniques calls mutation uniform and uniform crossover . These techniques generate new solutions to the combine and adjust solutions existing . The goal is to find solutions that are next best combination possible , known as Pareto frontier . To decide about the best food combination , we use the Gurobi software , which considers all information about you food and user preferences . This software helps you determine the ideal amount of each food at diet .

A equation below presents an example of a formulation Gurobi 's mathematics with the pre- selected nutrients . The formulation of the function goal *Max*   and   the sum of energy provided per each diet food ,

food , energy

considering the energy product per unit by the quantity of the respective food (22). The restrictions they are also formulated per one linear combination involving the quantity of each food (23). In addition to some boundary conditions associated with the diet formulation itself , the restrictions generally they are associated with values maximum and minimum nutrients and calories . Being so , *food , , 1< i <N,* are the decision variables (quantity of each food gift at solution candidate coming from NSGA-II) and each coefficient *c, 1<j< M* and 1 < *n<N* refers to concentration , for unit , of the nutrient *j* in *n* - th food , or any other variable that should meet some tolerance range .

$$Max_{alimentos,energia} : objetivo = \sum_{i=1}^{N} alimento_i energia_i \qquad (22)$$

s.t

$$calcio_1 alimento_1 + calcio_2 alimento_2 + ... + calcio_N alimento_N \geq calcio_{min}$$

$$calcio_1 alimento_1 + calcio_2 alimento_2 + ... + calcio_N alimento_N \leq calcio_{max}$$

$$proteina_1 alimento_1 + proteina_2 alimento_2 + ... + proteina_N alimento_N \geq proteina_{min}$$

$$proteina_1 alimento_1 + proteina_2 alimento_2 + ... + proteina_N alimento_N \leq proteina_{max}$$

$$sodio_1 alimento_1 + sodio_2 alimento_2 + ... + sodio_N alimento_N \geq sodio_{min}$$

$$sodio_1 alimento_1 + sodio_2 alimento_2 + ... + sodio_N alimento_N \leq sodio_{max}$$

$$fibra_1 alimento_1 + fibra_2 alimento_2 + ... + fibra_N alimento_N \geq fibraalimentar_{min}$$

$$fibra_1 alimento_1 + fibra_2 alimento_2 + ... + fibra_N alimento_N \leq fibraalimentar_{max}$$

$$ferro_1 alimento_1 + ferro_2 alimento_2 + ... + ferro_N alimento_N \geq ferro_{min}$$

$$ferro_1 alimento_1 + ferro_2 alimento_2 + ... + ferro_N alimento_N \leq ferro_{max}$$

$$vitaminaA_1 alimento_1 + vitaminaA_2 alimento_2 + ... + vitaminaA_N alimento_N \geq vitaminaA_{min}$$

$$vitaminaA_1 alimento_1 + vitaminaA_2 alimento_2 + ... + vitaminaA_N alimento_N \leq vitaminaA_{max}$$

$$(23)$$

Just as an example illustrative , Table 10 presents a result found for the Gurobi .

Variable	Quantity (1 unit = 100g)	Energy (kca)	Price (R$ per 100g)
SoluQao Candidate	43	6670.82	R$566.27

Whole Wheat Bread	1	253.19	R$7.59
Drink Dairy with Peach	7	55.16	R$5.50
Avocado	17	96.10	R$5.28
Cooked Brown Rice	7	123.53	R$5.28
Pumpkin Cabotian Stew	1	48.04	R$2.53
Presented	1	128.86	R$6.71
Lime Orange Juice	1	39.34	R$1.43
Peanut	4	554.05	R$6.05
Abadejo File Roast	1	111.62	R$0.44
Pumpkin Cabotian Stew	1	48.04	R$2.53
Dende Olive Oil	1	884.00	R$6.38
Avocado	1	96.15	R$5.28

Source: Own elaboration .

Table 10. Example of Gurobi Result .

It is implicit at figure the call to the Gurobi , which defines the quantity best of each food for all solutions candidates , in addition to evaluates the two objective functions of the diet problem , for all solutions candidates .

The Gurobi he has resources for dealing with multiple objectives (Gurobi , 2021), but not from the perspective of populating one Pareto frontier and generate diversity of solutions candidates , from different *trade-* offs between goals . What the Gurobi he can make and combine several objectives of a problem in a hierarchical way , defining one order of priority for multiple objectives and optimizing according to order established . Prioritize goals in sequence is not compatible with the type of problem here formulated for the diet to feed .

3.7 System result for diet food

The multi - objective recommendation system for diets food he was implemented under a optimization perspective bimable , with the support of NSGA-II and Gurobi *solvers* . Some results they are shown below , corresponding to solutions facUveis that present appointments different between the two higher - level objectives : total *cost* of food and organization of food distribution in the meals , called *concentration* . On the lower level , the Gurobi works with maximizing the total energy of the diet .

Consider the case of a diet to feed designed for a 25 year old man , which suggests four meals daily rates : Breakfast, Lunch , Dinner and Snack. Snack can be adapted according to the individual 's preference , being accomplished at Morning or afternoon . This diet specific proposes one variety of foods , distributed in 15 categories distinct , covering all meals .

In addition to specifying you types of food , diet also details you main nutrients necessary to meet the needs energy and nutrition of the individual . A crucial aspect of the diet is considering the cost of food . Given that the accessibility financial and a concern significant for the 25 year old man , the diet search balance you requirements nutritional with the viability economic .

Table 11 , which accompanies it is description , provides details complete about diet , including you types of food recommended for each meal , the nutrients key to be consumed , and a cost analysis to facilitate purchasing decisions . This table serves as a guide comprehensive to help at adherence to the diet , ensuring that all needs nutritional be served in an economical way .

Composition of the Dietary Diet	
Snack	**Composition**
Cafe da Manha (Caf)	Three Categories : Cereals , Milk, Fruits
Lunch (Alm)	Five Categories : Cereals , Legumes , Vegetables , Meat, Eggs
Dinner (Jan)	Four Categories : Drinks , Vegetables , Fish , Milk
Snack (Lan)	Three Foods: Vegetables , Milk, Fruits
Nutrients Selected	
[Energy , Price , Protein , Calcium, Sodium, Fiber Food , Iron, Vitamin A]	

Source: Own elaboration .

Table 11. Diet composition in food categories .

You nutrients gifts at diet are the restrictions imposed to the diet problem , in addition to energy and cost (energy and cost they are objective functions in the upper level , but restrictions in the lower level), totaling 9 elements for restrictions . However , the system works with restrictions maxima and minima , which leads to a total of 18 types of restrictions . You NSGA-II hyperparameters are :
- Population size : 100
- Number of generations : 10
- Crossover probability : 50%
• Uniform Crossover Operator
• Probability of mutation : 30%.
• Mutation Operator Uniform
• Tournament Selection Method
- 5 participant tournament
- Chance of victory for the strongest participant : 90%

Some definites they were placed in this example :
- Energy :
o Minimum : 2000 kcal
o Maximum: 6000 kcal
- Price :
o Minimum : R$10.00
o Maximum: R$500.00
- Food Portion : o 10 grams

initial settings of the system hyperparameters they were established based on literature references specialized . During the experimental tests , these configurations suffered settings aiming optimize system performance . It was observed that the combination of the NSGA-II and Gurobi algorithms resulted in improvements significant , especially up to the seventh or octave process generation evolutionary search .

As provided theoretically , the first process generations evolutionary demonstrated one higher rate of evolution of candidate solutions , aligned with the goals established for the search . He was identified that allow The population evolution for up to 10 generations enables development of the process , taking the solutions to a stage evolutionary more advanced and closer to ideal convergence .

Table 12, which accompanies This one document , presents a record detailed evolution of these candidate solutions in the search space , maintaining constant you hyperparameters initially settled down . This record offers valuable insights about

45

The effectiveness of optimization strategies adopted and serves as an important reference for future iterations and improvements to the system .

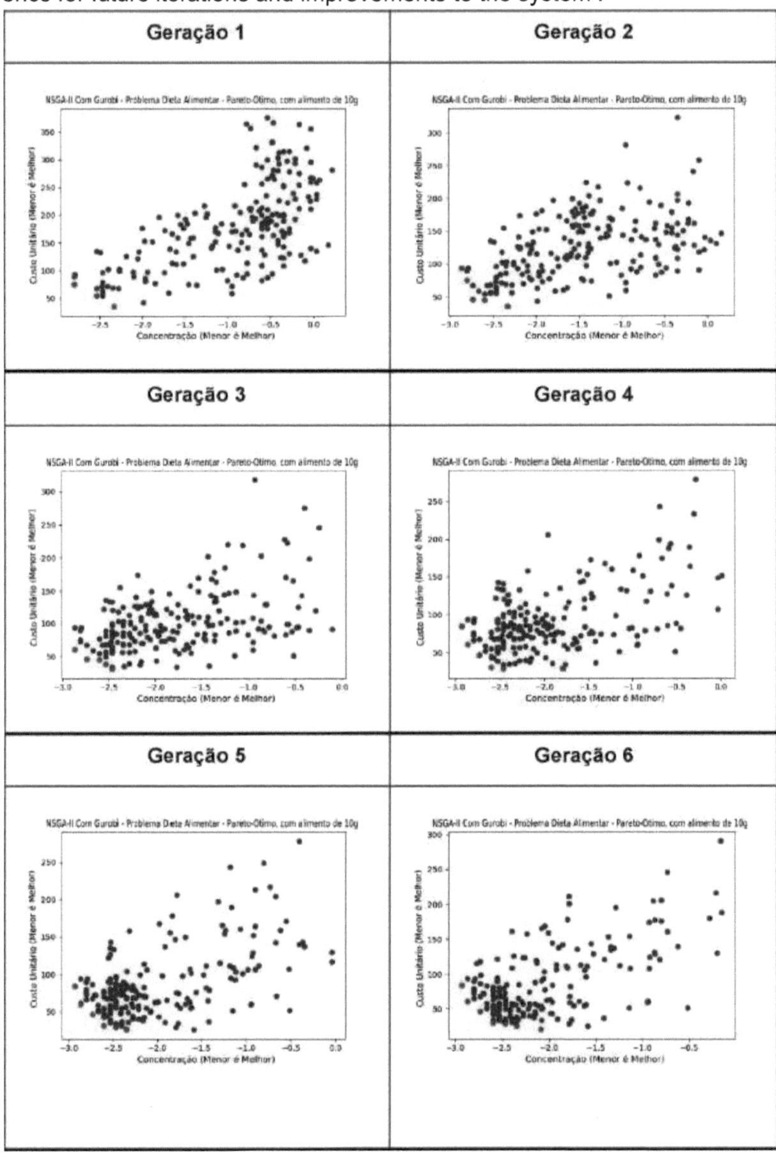

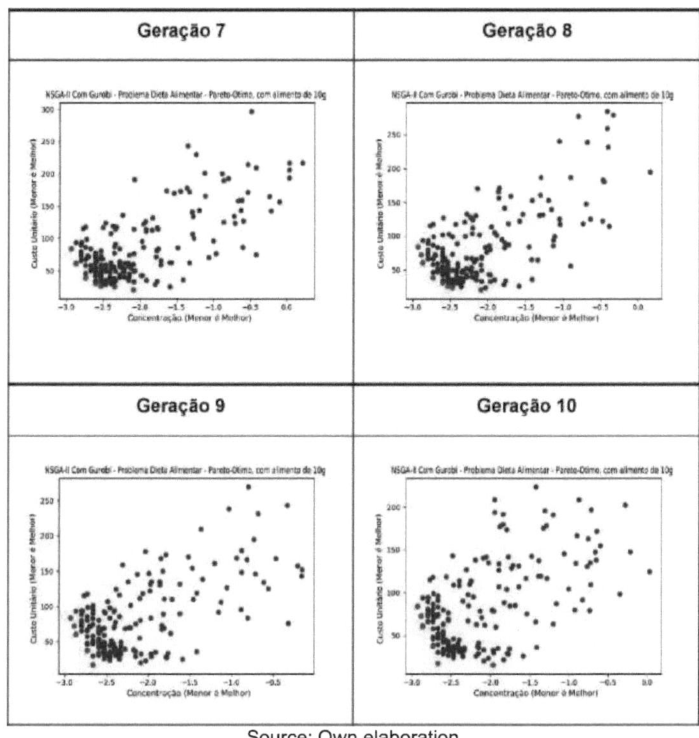

Source: Own elaboration

Table 12: Evolution of Solutions Candidates to the over 10 generations .

Figure 9 shows the search result at the end of the optimization process multi-objective bimvel , in which the points red are the solutions non-dominated (more close to the Pareto frontier), while you points blue are the solutions dominated . Table 13 contains you objectives of the four solutions found for the system and highlighted at Figure 9 , while Table 14 has the characteristics of these solutions . The first two (A and B) are solutions dominated , and the last two (C and D) are solutions non-dominated .

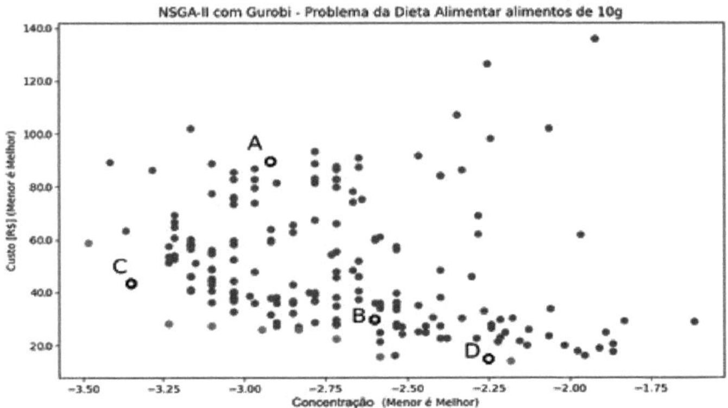

Source: Own elaboration .

Figure 9. Objective space (Cost x Concentration) with solutions candidates of the Dietary Problem (how much smaller you objective values , the better).

Solutions Candidates		Objectives of NSGA-II		Gurobi 's goal
		Price (R$)	Concentration	Energy (kcal
Solutions	A	86.94	-2.96	3900
Dominated	B	30.77	-2.65	3707
Non- Dominated	W	43.82	-3.35	2133
Solutions	D	15.18	-2.25	2031.38

Source: Own elaboration .

Table 13. Objectives of the four solutions candidates highlighted at Figure 8.

Solutions Dominated					
Solutions Candidates		Meal	Quantity (x10g)	Energy (kcal)	Price (R$)
A	Brown Rice	Breakfast	1	12.35	0.53
	Drink Peach Dairy		two	6.95	0.04
	Avocado		60	9.62	0.53
	Brown Rice	Lunch	1	12.35	0.53
	Peanut		1	54.40	0.60
	Cassava Farofa		1	40.51	0.25
	Beef		1	19.55	0.08
	Cheese omelet		52	26.80	0.19
	Cashew juice	To have	42	4.51	0.63
	Peanut	lunch	14	54.40	0.60
	Abadejo File		1	11.16	0.04
	Almond Toast		3	58.10	0.53
	Pumpkin Cabotian	Snack	1	4.80	0.26
	Babagu Oil		6	88.40	0.87
	Avocado		1	9.62	0.53
Solutions Candidates		Meal	Quantity (x10g)	Energy (kcal)	Price (R$)

48

	Solutions Candidates	Meal	Quantity (x10g)	Energy (kcal)	Price (R$)
B	Brown Rice	Breakfast	1	12.35	0.53
	Drink Peach Dairy		1	5.51	0.55
	Acai with Guarana Syrup		49	11.03	0.01
	Brown Rice	Lunch	1	12.35	0.52
	Peanut		1	54.40	0.60
	Pumpkin Cabotian		1	4.80	0.25
	Introduced		two	12.88	0.67
	Cheese omelet		51	26.80	0.18
	Grape juice	To have lunch	1	5.76	0.32
	Peanut		19	54.40	0.60
	Abadejo Filet		3	11.16	0.04
	Almond Toast		1	58.10	0.53
	Pumpkin	Snack	1	4.80	0.25
	Olive Oil (Oil)		6	88.40	0.64
	Canned Fig		1	18.43	0.85

<table>
<tr><td colspan="6" align="center">Non- Dominated Solutions</td></tr>
</table>

	Solutions Candidates	Meal	Quantity (x10g)	Energy (kcal)	Price (R$)
W	Brown Rice	Breakfast	1	12.35	0.53
	Pasteurized Cheese		23	25.66	0.06
	Khaki		20	7.13	0.18
	Curau Corn	Lunch	1	40.23	0.81
	Peanut		3	54.40	0.60
	Chard		37	2.09	0.36
	Presented		1	12.89	0.67
	Cheese omelet		two	26.80	0.19
	Cashew juice	To have lunch	3	4.51	0.63
	Peanut		1	54.40	0.60
	Abadejo File		1	11.16	0.04
	chestnut Brazil		10	64.30	0.56
	Pumpkin Cabotian	Snack	32	4.80	0.26
	Olive Oil (Oil)		1	88.40	0.64
	Avocado		8	9.62	0.53

	Solutions Candidates	Meal	Quantity (x10g)	Energy (kcal)	Price (R$)
D	Brown Rice	Breakfast	6	12.35	0.53
	Pasteurized Cheese		24	25.66	0.06
	Mage		1	5.55	0.23
	Brown Rice	Lunch	1	12.35	0.53
	Tremolo		19	38.13	0.09
	Cassava		3	15.14	0.03
	Presented		1	12.89	0.67
	Boiled Chicken Egg		1	14.57	0.80

Cashew juice	To have lunch	1	4.51	0.63
Peanut		3	54.40	0.60
Abadejo File		1	11.16	0.04
Almond		1	58.10	0.53
Pumpkin Cabotian	Snack	3	4.80	0.26
Olive Oil (Oil)		3	88.40	0.74
Avocado		1	9.62	0.53

Source: Own elaboration

Table 14. Solutions candidates highlighted at Figure 9.

observed that the joint work of two algorithms at optimization binrvel produced solutions non-dominated factweis and that approximate well on the Pareto frontier , in addition to exhibiting multiple *trade-* offs between two goals . You two goals they are indeed conflicting , characterizing good one Pareto frontier that establishes many different *trade-offs* between both.

Other observation relevant when analyzing these results and the effect caused by the absence of a specification more in agreement with the habits food Brazilians . Solutions A, B, C and D put boiled rice in the breakfast. Obviously there are people who like to eat rice in this meal , but it is not usual. The system he was designed to admit The inclusion of filters that force the occurrence or prevent the participation of food smart in meals smart , which, however , is not he was worked in this case study . Therefore, any food within a food category that is gift in one certain snack can be chosen with equal probability during the search .

You models mathematicians as essential tools to uncover and solve real world puzzles acquire one certain importance for societies . This book , therefore , does not just explore in depth you methods mathematicians more robust and recognized in the academic field , presenting the applications known that can to work in several strategies and scenarios different with the aim of helping people who have difficulties in follow one feeding healthy . But also the history and the challenges diet contemporaries food in Brazil and understanding the problem of diet food , which can be seen in more than one way, in addition to being a social problem , which needs solutions social issues , but a problem static , which can to bring results quantitative and qualitative , benefiting in the sockets decisions and helping people who need support to have one feeding healthy and safe .

As the complexity of a problem increases the creativity and complexity of the solution algorithm necessary to address it as well must to grow . This is particularly true in the case of the diet problem food , whose complexity go beyond the simple analysis of food costs and benefits , extending to aspects qualitative and nutritional . This book explored that need through a variety of approaches mathematics sophisticated , from The linear optimization up to algorithms evolutionary , offering to the readers one vision comprehensive and detailed techniques employed to resolve you challenges inherent to the diet problem to feed . In addition presentation of this work and a testimony that science it is constantly evolving , generating new methods and approaches that can improve the solution of classic problems . She highlighted as solutions creative , robust and innovative emerge to face challenges old , opening path to advancement significant in different areas of knowledge

References bibliographical

ANVISA. **Labeling Nutritional Mandatory** . Ministry of Health, University of Brasilia, 2005. Available at : <http://antigo.anvisa.gov. br/documents/33916/389979/Rotulagem+Nutricional+Obriga t%C3%B3ria+Manual+de+Orienta%C3%A7%C3%A3o+%C3%A0s+Ind%C3%BAstria s+de+Alimentos/ae72b30a-07af-42e2-8b76-10ff96b64ca4?version=1.0#page=27&zo om=auto,-194,580>. Acesso no dia 13 de Mar$o de 2021.

AMIN, Saman Hassanzadeh, MULLIGAN-GOW, Samantha, GUOQING, Zhang. **Selection of Food Items for Diet Problem Using a Multi-objective Approach Under Uncertainty.** Intechopen, 2019. Disponivel: <https://www.intechopen.com/books/application-of-decision-science-in-business-and-management/selection-of-food-items-for-diet-problem-using-a-multi-objective-approa ch-under-uncertainty>. Acesso no dia 18 de Setembro de 2020.

AMPL. **AMPL Development** . AMPL, 2023. Available at : < https://dev.ampl.com/? gl =1* yubvcm * ga*MiY0MjE1Mig0LjE2OTMyNTA3ODQ.* ga FY84K2YRRE*MTY5MzI1MDc4NC4xLiAuMTY5MzI1MDc4NC4wLjAuMA..& ga=2. 198591535.1488817305.1693250785-264215284.1693250784 >. Accessed on May 26 , 2023.

BAO, Pham Ngo Gia; QUAN, Tram Loi; THO, Quan Thanh; GARG, Akhil. **NSGA-II.** Ho Chi Minh University of Technology, 2018. Disponivel em: <https://github.com/baopng/NSGA-II>. Acesso no dia 15 de Julho de 2021.

BACK, Thomas., FOGEL, David B. & MICHALEWICZ, Zbigniew. **"Evolutionary Computation 1: Basic Algorithms and Operators"**, Institute of Physics Publishing, 2000.

BARBOSA, Geraldo Magela . **Using Linear Programming in Optimization of Production Results at Company . Sao Judas** University , Sao Paulo. 2014.

BARRE, Tangui; PERIGNON, Marlene; et al. *Integrating Nutrient Bioavailability and Co-production Links When Identifying Sustainable diets: How low should we reduce meat consumption?.* McMaster University, CANADA. 2018.

BEUME, Nicola; NAUJOKS, Naujoks; EMMERICH, Michael. **SMS-EMOA: Multiobjective Selection Based on Dominated Hypervolume.** European Journal of Operational Research, 2007.

CANADA. *Dietary Reference Intakes. Government of Canada, 2010.* Disponivel em: <https://www.canada.ca/en/health-canada/services/food-nutrition/healthy-eating/dieta ry-reference-intakes.html> . Acesso no dia 17 de Fevereiro de 2021.

CALLE, Paul. **NSGA-II explained.** Analytics lab @ OU, 2017. Available at : < http://oklahomaanalytics.com/data-science-techniques/nsga-ii-explained/ >. Accessed on July 15 , 2021.

CAVALLARO, Fausto. **A Takagi- Sugeno Fuzzy Inference System for Developing a Sustainability Index of Biomass.** Sustainability, 2015.

CARVALHO, Leonardo Barcha de. **Optimization Multipurpose in Shopping Route Problem .** Unicamp , Faculty of Engineering Electrical and Computing , 2014.

CASTRO, Josue de. **Geography of Hunger** . 10 ed. Rio de Janeiro, Edi^oes Antares, 1984. Available at : < https://o-geografo.webnode.com.br/_files/200000097-d07dcd177a/Jos%C3%BAe% 20de%20Castro%20Geografia%20da%20Fome.pdf >. Accessed on April 18 , 2022.

CEDERHOLM et al. **ESPEN guidelines on definitions and terminology of clinical nutrition** . Clinical Nutrition, vol. 36, pp. 49-64, 2017.

COELLO, Carlos A. **Evolutionary Multi-Objective Optimization: A Historical View of The Field.** IEEE Computational Intelligence Magazine, 2006.

DEB, Kalyanmoy. **Multi-Objective Optimization Using Evolutionary Algorithms: An Introduction.** Indian Institute of Technology Kanpur, 2011.

DEB, Kalyanmoy; PRATAP, Amrit; AGARWAL, Sameer; MEYARIVAN, T. **A Fast and Elitist Multiobjective Genetic Algorithm: NSGA-II.** IEEE Transactions on Evolutionary Computation, Vol. 6, 2002.

DOOREN, C Van. **A Review of the Use of Linear Programming to Optimize Diets, Nutritiously, Economically and Environmentally**, Frontiers in Nutrition, vol. 5, 48 pages, 2018.

EVERT et al. **Nutrition Therapy for Adults With Diabetes or Prediabetes: A Consensus Report**, Diabetes Care, vol. 42, no. 5, pp. 731–754,

FERREIRA, Estephany Menezes. **Multimodal and Multiobjective Recommendation^ao System For Diets Foods** Unicamp , GDP,

GASS, SI; HARRIS, CM. **Stigler's Diet Problem.** The Encyclopedia of Operations Research and Management Science , New York, NY , 2001 .

GEARHART, Jared L; ADAIR, Kristin L, DETRY, Richard J, et al. **Comparison of Open-Source Linear Programming Solvers**. Sandia National Laboratories, 2013. Acesso no dia 25 de Maio de 2023. Disponivel em: <https://blog.zhangzhk.com/files/Comparison-of-Open-Source-Linear-Programming-S olvers.pdf>.

GUROBI. ***Documentation.*** Gurobi Optimization, 2021. Disponivel em: < https://www.gurobi.com/documentation/ >. Accessed on January 3 , 2021. IBGE. **Health Portal, datasus** . Ministry of Health, 2021. Available at : < http://www2.datasus.gov.br/DATASUS/index.php >. Accessed on March 13 , 2021 .

JARDIM, Julia Gazzoni ; VIEIRA, Ricardo Augusto Mendonca; FERNANDES, Alberto Magno; ARAUJO, Raphael Pavesi; GLORIA, Leonardo Siqueira; JUNIOR, Nardele Moreno Rohem ; ROCHA, Norberto Silva; ABREU, Matheus Lima Correa. **Application of a Nonlinear Optimization Tool to Balance Diets With Constant Metabolizability** . University State of Norte Fluminense Darcy Ribeiro, 2013.

KALDIRIM, Elif; KOSE, Zekeriya. **Application Of A Multi-Objective Genetic Algorithm To The Modified Diet Problem.** Istanbul Technical University, 2006.

LIU, Risheng ; GAO, Jiaxin; ZHANG, Jin; MENG, Deyu ; LIN, Zhouchen . **Investigating Bi-Level Optimization for Learning and Vision from a Unified Perspective: A Survey and Beyond.** Journal of Latex, Cornell University, 2015.

MENDES, João Batista. **Approach Multiobjective for the Truck Dispatch Problem in Minas at Ceu Aberto. Federal** University of Minas Gerais, 2013.

MIRJALILI, Seyedali . **Genetic Algorithm. In: Evolutionary Algorithms and Neural Networks.** Studies in Computational Intelligence, vol 780, 2019. Publisher : Springer, Cham.

MS. **Food Guide for the Brazilian Population** . Ministry of Health, 2004. Available in : < https://cursosextensao.usp.br/pluginfile.php/47411/mod_resource/content/1/Orienta %C3%A7%C3%B5es%20Guia%20Alimentar.pdf >. Accessed on May 13 , 2021.

MISITANO, G; SAINI, B. S.; AFSAR, B.; SHAVAZIPOUR, B.; MIETTINEN, K. **DESDEO: The Modular and Open Source Framework for Interactive Multiobjective Optimization.** IEEE, 2021. Disponivel em: <https://ieeexplore.ieee.org/stamp/stamp.jsp?arnumber=9591595>. Acesso no dia 25 de Maio de 2023.

MIT, **Stigler, Diet Problem.** Massachusetts Institute of Technology , 2023. Available at : < https://blossoms.mit.edu/sites/default/files/video/download/Topcu-Stigler-Diet-Proble m.pdf https://www.mpi-inf.mpg.de/fileadmin/inf/d1/teaching/winter18/Ideen/Materialien/Dantzig-Diet .pdf >. Accessed on May 25 , 2023.

MUTHEE, Arthur. **The Basics of Genetic Algorithms in Machine Learning.** Section, 2021.

Available at : < https://www.section.io/engineering-education/the-basics-of-genetic-algorithms-in-ml/ >. Accessed on November 24 , 2021.

MYFITNESSPAL, **Lose weight with MyFitnessPal.com.** *MyFitnessPal, Inc, 2022.* Available at : < https://www.myfitnesspal.com/pt/welcome/learn_more >. Accessed on March 20 , 2022.

NCBI. *Dietary Reference Intakes.* National Center for Biotechnology Information, US, 2011. Available at : < https://www.ncbi.nlm.nih.gov/ >. Accessed on May 11 , 2020.

NEPA. **Brazilian Food Composition Table** . Studies and Research Center in Alimentagao , 2011. Available at : < https://www.cfn.org.br/wp-content/uploads/2017/03/taco_4_edicao_ampliada_e_revised.pdf >. Accessed on February 4 , 2021.

NUTRIGENIE. **Nutrition Software for Better Health.** *Stanford University,* US, 1991. Available at : < http://nutrigenie.biz/about.html >. Accessed on March 20 , 2022.

OBITKO, Marek. **Introduction to Genetic Algorithms.** University of Sciences Dresden Applied Sciences , 1998. Available at : < https://www.obitko.com/tutorials/genetic-algorithms/index.php >. Accessed on November 27 , 2021.

OLIVEIRA, Ricardo; CALDEIRA, Jefferson; TRATTNER, Christoph; MARINHO, Leandro Balby. Healthy Menus Recommendation: **Optimizing the Use of the Pantry. Conference: Workshop on Health Recommender Systems**, Canada, 2018. Disponivel em: <https://www.researchgate.net/publication/328450699_Healthy_Menus_Recommendation_Optimizing_the_Use_of_the_Pantry>. Acesso no dia 02 de Dezembro de 2021.

PATIL, Amol Nayakappa; KASTURI, Sidharth. *Optimal Diet Decision Using Linear Programming.* International Research Journal of Engineering and Technology, 2016.

RAIMUNDO, Marcos Medeiros. **An Extension to the Routing and Inventory Problem** . Master 's Thesis , Faculty of Engineering Electrical and Computing , Unicamp , 2014.

RESZELEWSKI, Wojciech; MIELNIK, Kamil. **NSGA-II** . Github , 2016. Available at : < https://github.com/wreszelewski/nsga2 >. Accessed on July 15 , 2021.

SA, Joao Luiz da Silva. **Hunger in Brazil : From the Colonial Period to 1940.** Revista de Geografia, 2006. Available in : <https://periodicos.ufpe.br/revistas/revistageografia/article/view/228669>. Acesso no dia 24 de Janeiro de 2021.

SANTOS, Quenia dos; SICHIERI, Rosely; DARMON, Nicole, MAILLOT, Malthieu; JUNIOR, Eliseu Verly-. **Food Choice to Meet Nutrient Recommendations for the Adult Brazilian Population Based on the Linear Programming Approach.** *Public Health Nutrition,* Cambridge University Press (CUP), 2018.

SINHA, A., MALO, P., DEB, K. **A Review on Bilevel Optimization: From Classical to Evolutionary Approaches and Applications**, IEEE Transactions on Evolutionary Computation, vol. 22, no. 2, pp. 276-295, 2018.

SOMMERVILLE, Ian. **Engenharia de Software.** Pearson Education do Brasil, 9ª Edi^ao, 2011.

SKLAN, David; DARIEL, Ilana. **Diet Planning For Humans Using Mixed-Integer Linear Programming.** Faculty of Agriculture, Hebrew University, 1992.

UPS. **Algorithms Genetics** . Institute of Sciences Mathematics and Computing at the University of São Paulo, 2021. Available at : < https://sites.icmc.usp.br/andre/research/genetic/ >. Accessed on November 20 , 2021.

SYDOW, Lexi. **Huge demand for workout guides, contact tracers and wellness apps as consumers try to stay healthy and safe at home.** Data.ia, 2021. Acesso no dia 25 de Maio de 2023.

UAB. **PerfectBody - Frequently Asked Questions - What is a Perfect Body Nutrition plan?** UAB "Kilo Group", 2022. Disponivel em: <https://perfectbody.me/faq>. Acesso no dia

21 de Mar$o de 2022.

USP. **Algorithms Genetics .** USP, 2021. Available in :
< https://sites.icmc.usp.br/andre/research/genetic/ >. Accessed on May 13 , 2021.

VASCONCELOS, Francisco de Assis Guedes de. **Josue de Castro and the Geography of Hunger in Brazil** . FORUM, 2008. Available at : < http://www.scielo.br/pdf/csp/v24n11/27.pdf >. Accessed on April 1 , 2021.

VASCONCELOS, Ivana Aragao L.; SOUSA, Maria Fatima de; SANTOS, Leonor Maria Pacheco. **Evolution of the number of nutritionists at Primary Care in Brazil : the contribution of the Family Health Support Centers and the Family Health Strategy from 2007 to 2013.** Revista de Nutrição , 2015. Available in :
< https://www ₁ scielo ᵢ br/j/rn/a/4RNW73cSs6QWqhm3qZGhQCy/?lang=pt# >. Access on May 26 , 2023.

VELDHUIZEN, David A. Van. **Multiobjective Evolutionary Algorithms: Classifications, Analyzes and New Innovations.** Air Force Institute of Technology, 1999. Available at : < https://apps.dtic.mil/sti/citations/ADA364478 >. Accessed on April 8 , 2021.

VIEUX, Florent; MAILLOT, Malthieu; RHEM, Colin D.; DREWNOWSKI, Adam. **Designing Optimal Breakfast for the United States Using Linear Programming and NHANES 2011-2014 Database. A Study from the International Breakfast Research Initiative (IBRI).** Breakfast Research Initiative (IBRI). *Nutrients,* 2019.

WHO. **Obesity.** World Health Organization, 2021. Disponivel em: <https://www.who.int/health-topics/obesity, 2021>. Acesso no dia 2 de Dezembro de 2021.

ZHENKUI, Pei; ZHEN, Liu. **Nutritional Diet Using Multi-Objective Difference Evolutionary Algorithm.** International Conference On Computational Intelligence and Natural Computing, 2009.

ZITZLER, Eckart; LAUMANNS, Marco; THIELE, Lothar. SPEA2: **Improving the strength pareto evolutionary algorithm,** Technical Report ETH Zurich, 2001.

Buy your books fast and straightforward online - at one of world's fastest growing online book stores! Environmentally sound due to Print-on-Demand technologies.

Buy your books online at
www.morebooks.shop

Kaufen Sie Ihre Bücher schnell und unkompliziert online – auf einer der am schnellsten wachsenden Buchhandelsplattformen weltweit! Dank Print-On-Demand umwelt- und ressourcenschonend produzi ert.

Bücher schneller online kaufen
www.morebooks.shop

Printed by Books on Demand GmbH, Norderstedt / Germany